D0641630

Exploring Math
with Books Kids Love

Kathryn Kaczmarski

fulcrum resources
Golden, Colorado

Text and cover design by Dovetail Publishing Services
Illustrations by Dovetail Publishing Services

Library of Congress Cataloging-in-Publication Data

Kaczmarski, Kathryn.
    Exploring math with books kids love / Kathryn Kaczmarski.
      p. cm.
    Includes bibliographical references and index.
    ISBN 1-55591-960-X
    1. Mathematics teachers—Training of. 2. Mathematics—Study and teaching (Elementary).
  3. Mathematics—Study and teaching (Elementary)—Activity programs. 4. Curriculum planning.
  5. Mathematics in literature. I. Title.
    QA135.5K14   1998
    372.7'044—dc21
                                                    98-28326
                                                      CIP

Credits
Page 14: Pages 215–217 of *The Pushcart War* by Jean Merrill, 1964 used by permission of HarperCollins Publishers.
Pages 36–43: Excerpts from *The Phantom Tollbooth* by Norton Juster. Copyright © 1961 and renewed 1989 by Normon Juster. Reprinted by permission of Random House, Inc.
Page 60: Thanks to The Red Lantern Restaurant in Arvada, Colorado, for permission to reprint their menu.
Page 122: The INS graph on page 29 of *The Challenge of Immigration* by Vic Cox, 1995, is used by permission of Enslow Publishers, Inc.
Pages 180–183: The *NCTM Standards from Curriculum and Evaluation Standards for School Mathematics* copyright 1989 is reprinted by permission of the National Council of Teachers of Mathematics. All rights reserved.

Printed in the United States of America
0 9 8 7 6 5 4 3 2 1

Fulcrum Publishing
350 Indiana Street, Suite 350
Golden, Colorado 80401-5093
(800) 992-2908 • (303) 277-1623
website: www.fulcrum-resources.com
e-mail: fulcrum@fulcrum-resources.com

Contents

Introduction

If you had ever watched me teach, you might have thought that I got off the subject too often. However, what was important to me was not "the subject," but the education of my students. If I had an opportunity to teach a mathematical concept that came up in a book or poem during language arts, great. If my students could learn an historical or sociological lesson during math, so much the better. Life is not bundled up in tidy one-hour increments where we can handle one narrow facet of it before moving on to the next. Life itself is an integrated curriculum; it is impossible to tell where one discipline ends and another begins. I have even found it nearly impossible to divide this book up into tidy separations. A novel may be listed in one chapter but may certainly contain lessons that belong in several others. My aim in writing this book is to give teachers interested in integrating curriculum a few ideas with which to begin.

Novels for this age group are the most commonly used resource, but nonfiction and a few poems are also included. You will see that mathematics and language arts are not the only subjects integrated in this work. You will also find topics such as art and architecture, history, sociology, geography, science, economics, and current events.

Every standard listed for grades 5–8 in the *Curriculum and Evaluation Standards for School Mathematics* by the National Council of Teachers of Mathematics (1989) is used somewhere in this book. Each section indicates which standards (or parts of standards) are used in that book. (See the Index for references to specific standards and the Appendix for a complete list of the NCTM Standards.)

Who Is This Book For?

- Intermediate and middle school teachers interested in integrating curriculum

- Homeschooling parents needing new ideas and ways to teach children of different grade levels at the same time

- Teachers of gifted students looking for new challenges

How to Use This Book

Give yourself a break—start as small as you want. There is no need to block out a daily time period for a new class in which you teach math and language arts together. There is no need to throw away your math text or your current reading list. See if one of the novels you already read with or to your class is included in this book, and try a few ideas presented here. Or look in the index for a math topic that you will be teaching soon. Perhaps you can add a new activity or presentation technique. For easy use, reproducible worksheets are provided, and the answers to many questions are enclosed in brackets in the text.

Kill two birds with one stone. Many of the lessons included here require that students write. Some exercises use the writing process. Why spend time developing writing assignments when students can write in content areas?

Do not dismiss any of the lessons as too easy or too hard for your students. Some lessons are presented using picture books; they are not meant only for younger students. In fact, I would not hesitate to use them with adults. Some lessons may include math problems that are too difficult for your students. See if you can use the lesson, but substitute the actual math work with problems at a level more appropriate for your students.

As your comfort level grows, you will find that integrating curriculum is not only a more interesting way to teach, but is also more efficient.

Acknowledgments

Deepest appreciation goes to Jerry Kaczmarski for his computer assistance and loving support, not necessarily in that order, and not necessarily given simultaneously; to James Kaczmarski for his mathematical assistance; and to Jonathan and Micah Kaczmarski who will get their feelings hurt if I neglect to mention them.

1

Number Relationships, Systems, and Theory

How Much Is a Million?

by David M. Schwartz
New York: Lothrop, Lee, & Shepherd Books, 1985

The concepts of very large numbers—a million, a billion, a trillion—are difficult to understand. This book attempts to give meaning to large numbers through comparisons and illustrations.

Although *How Much Is a Million?* is classified as juvenile literature and is published in picture-book format, middle-grade students can benefit from reading, seeing, or hearing this book. They often have trouble conceptualizing large numbers and need new ways to think about magnitude.

Topic Large numbers

Objective To understand the magnitude of large numbers

Applicable NCTM Standards 1, 2, 4, 5, 6, 7, 8

Visualizing Large Numbers

To help us visualize a million stars, the illustrator of *How Much Is a Million?*, Steven Kellogg, has drawn seven pages of stars. In order to see a million stars, these pages must be looked at ten times. Because there are 100,548 stars on the pages, ten times this amount is more than a million—1,005,480.

1. How many stars would you put on each of seven pages (to be viewed ten times) to make the amount closer to one million?   [Sample answer: 14,286 because 1,000,000 ÷ 70 ≈ 14,285.71; 14,286 stars × 7 pages × 10 viewings = 1,000,020 stars.]

2. How could you arrange these stars in an array on each page? How many would go across each row and how many would go down in each column?
    [Answers will vary. Sample answers: (1) 119 stars across and down would equal 14,161 stars per page; 14,161 × 7 pages × 10 viewings = 991,270 stars. (2) 120 stars across and down would equal 14,440 stars per page; 14,440 × 7 × 10 = 1,008,000 stars.]

3. If you put the stars on ten pages to be viewed ten times, how many stars would need to go on each page to view one million?   [10,000: 10,000 × 10 × 10 = 1,000,000]

4. How could the stars be arranged in an array on each page?
    [Sample answer: 100 across and 100 down: 100 × 100 = 10,000]

Spending Millions

Solve the following problems. Show all numerical work and write an explanation of your thinking and mathematical process.

1. If your mother gives you a million dollars and tells you to go spend $1000 a day, about how long will you be gone?   [2.7 years or about 3 years]

2. If she gives you a billion dollars and tells you to go spend $1000 a day, about how long will you be gone?   [about 3000 years]

Counting to a Million

A man in Wyoming spent years counting millions on his calculator (one plus one plus one plus one ...). It took him 5 years to count his first million. After he got faster, it took him 436 days to count to a million.

1. About how much did he count each day?   [about 2294: 1,000,000 ÷ 436 ~ 2293.58]

2. He made 5790 mistakes counting his last million. About how often did he make an error?   [about once every 173 numbers: 1,000,000 ÷ 5790 ≈ 172.71]

3. Why would someone do this?   [Any guess is as good as another.]

The National Debt

In 1996 the U.S. government was in great debt. The Federal government owed $5.6 trillion. (If students show interest, have them research how the debt was accumulated.)

1. How is 5.6 trillion written numerically?   [5,600,000,000,000]

2. How is 5.6 billion written numerically? 5.6 million?   [5,600,000,000; 5,600,000]

3. How many times greater is 5,600,000,000,000 than 5,600,000?   [1,000,000 times greater]

4. If your mother gives you $5.6 trillion (like the national debt) and tells you to go spend $1000 a day, about how long will you be gone?   [about 15,342,466 years]

Out of This World Calculations

Look at the end of *How Much Is a Million?* to see how David Schwartz explains how he made the calculations for this book. One thing he says is that a trillion kids standing on top of each other would reach 758 million miles—as far as Saturn's rings.

1. How far would 5.6 trillion kids standing on top of each other reach?
    [over 4 billion miles: 758,000,000 × 5.6 = 4,244,800,000]

2. How far into the solar system would these kids reach?   [737,700,000 miles past Pluto!]

Imagine those kids standing on each others' shoulders extending a 737.7 million miles past Pluto. Now imagine that each one is holding one dollar. If each kid gives his dollar to the U.S. government, it could pay back all the money it owes!

Big Words for Big Numbers

On the back cover of *How Much Is a Million?*, this question is asked: How much is a zillion? Look up the word "zillion" in the dictionary. How much is it? How about the word "gazillion"? What are some other words people use for very large numbers? Give each student a copy of Figure 1.1, How Big Are They?, which shows actual large numbers.

   In Great Britain they use they use the term "million" the same way we do. But they call a thousand millions a milliard. We call it a billion. Their billion is a million millions—a one followed by twelve zeros. Our trillion is just a thousand billions, but their trillion is a million billions—a one followed by fifteen zeros. Give each student a copy of Figure 1.2, British Names for Large Numbers.

1.   How does the British system compare to ours? What is the pattern?   [Some students might say, "Our periods go up by three zeros each time; theirs go up by six." Students with a better understanding may say, "In our system each period is a thousand times greater than the one before. In the British system, each period is a million times greater than the one before."]

2.   Do you see a pattern in the naming of British numbers? Do the prefixes of the numbers—bi-, tri-, quad-, quint-, and so on—have any relationship to their names? Look up the meanings of the prefixes in a dictionary if you do not know them. Can you see a pattern that would relate the prefixes to the written number?

Hint Rename each period using only 1,000,000 as a factor.

- million = 1,000,000
- billion = 1,000,000 × 1,000,000
- trillion = 1,000,000 × 1,000,000 × 1,000,000
- quadrillion = 1,000,000 × 1,000,000 × 1,000,000 × 1,000,000

[*Bi*llion uses 1,000,000 as a factor *two* times, *tri*llion uses 1,000,000 as a factor *three* times, *quadr*illion uses 1,000,000 as a factor *four* times, ...]

Scientific Notation

People who work with very large numbers, such as mathematicians and scientists, don't want to waste time writing out lots of zeros. Also, very large numbers take up too much room and are messy to work with. That is why the system of scientific notation was devised. Scientific notation allows very large numbers to be written in a shortened way. To understand scientific notation you first must understand factors and exponents.

1.   Rename the following numbers using only factors of ten.

a.   100   [10 × 10]

b.   1000   [10 × 10 × 10]

c.   10,000   [10 × 10 × 10 × 10]

d.   100,000   [10 × 10 × 10 × 10 × 10]

e.   1,000,000   [10 × 10 × 10 × 10 × 10 × 10]

Figure 1.1 Reproducible
How Big Are They?*

Thousand	1,000
Million	1,000,000
Billion	1,000,000,000
Trillion	1,000,000,000,000
Quadrillion	1,000,000,000,000,000
Quintillion	1,000,000,000,000,000,000
Sextillion	1,000,000,000,000,000,000,000
Septillion	1,000,000,000,000,000,000,000,000
Octillion	1,000,000,000,000,000,000,000,000,000
Nonillion	1,000,000,000,000,000,000,000,000,000,000
Decillion	1,000,000,000,000,000,000,000,000,000,000,000
Undecillion	1,000,000,000,000,000,000,000,000,000,000,000,000
Duodecillion	1,000,000,000,000,000,000,000,000,000,000,000,000,000
Tredecillion	1,000,000,000,000,000,000,000,000,000,000,000,000,000,000
Quattuordecillion	1,000,000,000,000,000,000,000,000,000,000,000,000,000,000,000
Quindecillion	1,000,000,000,000,000,000,000,000,000,000,000,000,000,000,000,000
Sexdecillion	1,000,000,000,000,000,000,000,000,000,000,000,000,000,000,000,000,000
Septendecillion	1,000,000,000,000,000,000,000,000,000,000,000,000,000,000,000,000,000,000
Octodecillion	1,000,000,000,000,000,000,000,000,000,000,000,000,000,000,000,000,000,000,000
Novemdecillion	1,000,000,000,000,000,000,000,000,000,000,000,000,000,000,000,000,000,000,000,000
Vigintillion	1,000,000,000,000,000,000,000,000,000,000,000,000,000,000,000,000,000,000,000,000,000
Googol	10,000,000,000,000,000,000,000,000,000,000,000,000,000,000,000,000,000,000,000,000,000,000,000,000,000,000,000,000,000,000,000,000,000,000

*France also uses this system.

Figure 1.2 Reproducible
British Names for Large Numbers*

Million   1,000,000

Milliard   1,000,000,000

Billion   1,000,000,000,000

Trillion   1,000,000,000,000,000,000

Quadrillion 1,000,000,000,000,000,000,000,000

Quintillion 1,000,000,000,000,000,000,000,000,000,000

Sextillion   1,000,000,000,000,000,000,000,000,000,000,000,000

Septillion   1,000,000,000,000,000,000,000,000,000,000,000,000,000,000

Octillion   1,000,000,000,000,000,000,000,000,000,000,000,000,000,000,000,000

Nonillion   1,000,000,000,000,000,000,000,000,000,000,000,000,000,000,000,000,000,000

Decillion   1,000,000,000,000,000,000,000,000,000,000,000,000,000,000,000,000,000,000,000,000

*Germany also uses this system.

2. Another way to write 10×10 is 10^2. The raised numeral is called an exponent. It indicates how many times the factor is used. For instance, 1,000,000, or $10 \times 10 \times 10 \times 10 \times 10 \times 10$, can be written as 10^6, which is read "ten to the sixth power." Here are some numbers renamed with exponents:

    - $1 = 10^0$

    - $10 = 10^1$

    - $100 = 10^2$

    - $1000 = 10^3$

    - $10,000 = 10^4$

    - $100,000 = 10^5$

    - $1,000,000 = 10^6$

    What is the pattern?   [The number of zeros equals the exponent.]

3. Not all scientific numbers can be written as factors of ten alone, but they can be renamed in a way to use powers of ten. For example:

    - $3,000,000 = 3 \times 1,000,000 = 3 \times 10^6$

    - $70,000,000,000 = 7 \times 10,000,000,000 = 7 \times 10^{10}$

    The first factor must be greater than or equal to one and less than ten; thus 70,000,000,000 cannot be written as 70×10^9. Use scientific notation to rename these numbers:

    a.   600,000,000   [6×10^8]

    b.   200,000   [2×10^5]

    c.   400,000,000,000   [4×10^{11}]

4. Not all scientific numbers are as tidy as the ones above—a single digit followed by lots of zeros. The Moon is about 239,000 miles from Earth. The number 239,000 can be written in scientific notation as 2.39×10^5. Venus is about 67,000,000 miles from the Sun. In scientific notation that is written as 6.7×10^7. Study these examples:

    - $560,000,000 = 5.6 \times 10^8$

    - $14,360,000 = 1.436 \times 10^7$

    - $2200 = 2.2 \times 10^3$

    - $3,270,000,000 = 3.27 \times 10^9$

    Do you see a pattern for renaming large numbers in scientific notation?
    [Answers will vary, but should be something like, "Put a decimal point after the first number, count how many places are after that, and use that number as the exponent of 10."]

5. Here are the rules for writing numbers in scientific notation:

   - The first factor must be greater to or equal to one and less than ten.

   - The second factor is a power of ten written with an exponent (written in exponential form).

   - Count the number of places to the right of the first number. That is the exponent.

   Write the following numbers in scientific notation:

   a.   631,100,000   [6.31×10^7]

   b.   94,000   [9.4×10^4]

   c.   417,800,000,000   [4.178×10^{11}]

   Write the following numbers in standard form.

   d. 8.1×10^4 [81,000]

   e. 9×10^8 [900,000,000]

   f. 4.64×10^7 [46,400,000]

   What process did you use? How did you "undo" scientific notation?

6. Very small numbers also can be written in scientific notation. Study these examples and figure out the procedure.

   - .00000000002 = 2×10^{-11} (Read this as "two times ten to the negative eleventh power.")

   - .00055 = 5.5×10^{-4}

   - .000000381 = 3.81×10^{-7}

   What is the pattern or process?

   - The first factor is greater than or equal to one and less than ten.

   - The second factor is a negative power of ten written in exponential form.

   - Count the number of places to the right of the decimal point including the first number that is not zero. That number of places becomes the negative exponent.

7. Rewrite the small numbers below in scientific notation.

   a.   .000097   [9.7×10^{-5}]

   b.   .00044   [4.4×10^{-4}]

   c.   .00000000246   [2.46×10^{-9}]

8. At one time astronomers concluded that there were 50 billion galaxies in the universe. Write 50 billion in standard form and in scientific notation. [50,000,000,000 = 5×10^{10}]

9. Astronomers estimated that with 50 to 100 billion stars per galaxy, the number of stars in the universe could be 5,000,000,000,000,000,000,000. Write the number of stars in words and in scientific notation. [five sextillion = 5×10^{21}]

For Your Amazement

How long would it take to visit 50 billion galaxies? (A traveler who spends one second in each galaxy, 24 hours a day, 365 days a year, would go through them all in 1585 years, 5 months, 28 days, 16 hours, and 37 minutes.)

To Think About

What is in space beyond the last galaxy? Can nothingness exist?

"How Much Is a Million?" Class Project

To see what a million of something actually looks like, try to collect a million objects in one year. Have students brainstorm ideas for these questions: What could we collect a million of this year? How long would it take? (Typically underestimated— "Four months?") What should we do with the items when we are done? (Some classes come up with altruistic uses.) Below are examples of what some students have done.

- In 1995 students in a New Jersey classroom collected one million buttons between the months of January and June.

- One class collected tea bag tags. They tied the project into geography by studying tea-drinking countries, tea-growing countries, and the places the tags originated. Long into the project, they estimated that at their collection rate it would take 4 to 5 years to reach one million.

- It took another class 15 months to collect a million pennies. The students signed up sponsors, ran laps, stacked wood, cared for pets, and raided their piggy banks. They donated the $10,000 (the equivalent of one million pennies) to the Nature Conservancy to save a local wetland area.

- One class collected the pull tabs from aluminum beverage cans estimating that they could complete the project in 4 months. Actually, the students collected about 250,000 tabs a year. After 3 years (and three different classes) the pull tabs were sold to an aluminum recycler who reluctantly bought them. The money was used to buy rain forest acreage to protect it from being destroyed.

Related Books

Coerr, Eleanor. *Sadako and the Thousand Paper Cranes.* New York: Putnam Publishing Group, 1977.

Guinness Book of Records. New York: Bantam Books, yearly.

Manes, Stephen. *Make Four Million Dollars by Next Thursday!* New York: Bantam Doubleday Dell Books for Young Readers, 1992.

Merrill, Jean. *The Toothpaste Millionaire.* Boston: Houghton Mifflin Company, 1972.

Rockwell, Thomas. *How to Get Fabulously Rich.* New York: Dell Yearling, 1990.

The World Almanac and Book of Facts. Mahwah, New Jersey: World Almanac Books, yearly.

Math Curse

by Jon Scieszka and Lane Smith
New York: Viking, 1995

In this story, Mrs. Fibonacci tells her students that almost everything can be seen as a math problem. One girl feels she is under a math curse: Why must math infiltrate every area of her life? Although this book is written in picture-book format, it is intended for "ages >6 and <99." It is an excellent book to read aloud to students of all ages. Read the book all the way through to give listeners a chance to enjoy the humor and story line. Then go back and use any or all pages to teach, reinforce, or extend math concepts.

Topics Number patterns and relationships, variety of other math topics

Objective To extend simple math concepts to more difficult levels

Applicable NCTM Standards 1, 2, 3, 4, 5, 6, 7, 8, 11

Working with Math in *Math Curse*

Math is integrated throughout this book. The following problems are just a few the frontmatter of this book would inspire.

1. The price of the 1995 edition of this book is [($3.25 + $1.75) × 3] + $1.99 = $16.99. Write three different multistep ways to calculate $16.99. Each example must include multiplication or division. See page 41 of this book for the rules regarding order of operations. Mathematicians have agreed that multistep problems must be done in a certain order to insure that everyone arrives at the same solution.

2. This book is for ages >6 and <99. Is it for six-year-olds? ninety-nine–year–olds? [No, greater than 6 does not include 6 and less than 99 does not include 99.]

3. How many ages is the book for?   [7 through 98 or 92]

4. The copyright is MCMXCV. What year is this?   [1995]

5. Work the math in the dedications, then write a similar mathematical dedication for an imaginary (or real) book you have written. Make it complicated enough that another student will be challenged while seeking the solution.

Exploring Combinations

The girl in the *Math Curse* cannot decide which shirt to wear to school. She has one white shirt, three blue shirts, three striped shirts, and one ugly plaid shirt from Uncle Zeno. If she also has one pair of blue jeans and one pair of white slacks, from how many possible combinations must she decide? (Assume that every striped shirt and every blue shirt is different from the others.) [16 combinations] Draw a tree diagram.

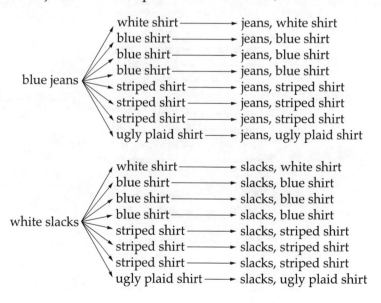

More Practice with Combinations

1. Rachel and Rafael want to see a movie and to get something to eat afterward. They have narrowed their movie choices to *Maybe Next Time*, *Nine Dead Men*, and *Terror*. They like pizza, tacos, and hamburgers. How many possible combinations do they have for their activity?   [9 combinations]

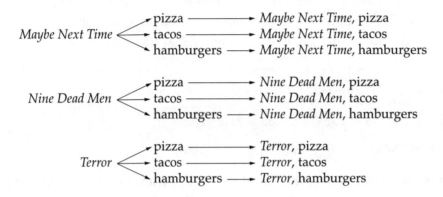

2. You are playing a card game with a friend. There are two piles of cards. Each pile has only four cards in it—a jack, a queen, a king, and an ace. You can draw one card from each pile. The order in which the cards are drawn is important. Draw a tree diagram to find all the possible combinations. How many are there? [16 combinations]

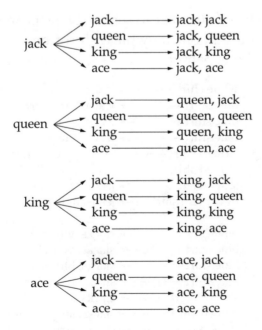

3. In the next card game it does not make any difference in what order the cards are drawn. Now how many combinations are there? (Any repeat of a combination can be eliminated—for example, jack/king is the same as king/jack.) [10 combinations]

4. When order does not make any difference, it is called a combination. When order does matter, it is called a permutation. Which card game above is a permutation? [first game]

Practice Writing Math Problems

After the math-cursed student chooses an outfit from one of the combinations, she frets over her breakfast. Can you make up math problems like hers that will make people laugh?

Exploring Estimation

The math-cursed student doesn't want to know how many flakes are in her cereal bowl. What would be an easy way to estimate the number of flakes in a whole box of cereal? [Sample answers: (1) Measure out one serving of cereal. The serving size is listed on the side of the box and is usually $3/4$ or one cup. Count the flakes in one serving and multiply by the number of servings per box. (2) To simplify the procedure, measure and count half a serving: $1/2$ of $3/4$ cup is $1/2 \times 3/4$, or $3/8$ cup. (A simple way to measure $3/8$ cup is $1/4$ cup plus 2 tablespoons.) Multiply that count by 2 to estimate the number of flakes in a whole serving, and then multiply that product by the number of servings per box. (3) Measure 1 ounce of cereal on a food scale and count the flakes in an ounce. Multiply the number of flakes in an ounce by the number of ounces of cereal in the box.]

Having Fun with Story Problems

The authors make fun of story problems throughout this book. What are some incongruencies—things that don't make sense—in the bus problem? [The question presented in the bus problem has nothing to do with the information given. The question cannot be answered true or false.]

Scieszka and Smith are not the only authors to have fun with word problems. In *The Pushcart War* by Jean Merrill (1964), New York pushcart vendors and truck drivers try to sabotage each other, each group believing the other is a public nuisance. At the end of the book, Frank the Flower [vendor] develops a mathematical solution to the problem (pages 215–217). Find all examples of faulty reasoning in Frank's solution. Here is the formula and explanation as it appears in *The Pushcart War**:

If: T = trucks
And: t = time
Then: ½ T = ½ t

The example given with the formula … is the same one that was originally presented to the Pushcart Peace Conference:

If: there are 100,000 trucks (100,000 T) in the city, traffic will be so bad that it will take 10 hours (10 t) to deliver a load of potatoes from 1st Street to 100th Street.

But if: there are only ½ as many trucks (50,000 T), traffic will only be ½ as bad, and it will take only ½ as long (5 t) to deliver a load of potatoes from 1st Street to 100th Street.

Therefore: One truck can make two trips in one day.

Which means: 50,000 trucks making two trips a day can deliver as many potatoes as 100,000 trucks making one trip.

Moreover: If the potato dealer is paying the truckers by the hour, he will be getting two loads delivered for the price of one.

Thus: He can sell the potatoes for less (which his customers will appreciate).

Result: Everybody (including pushcart peddlers) will be happier.

Professor Lyman Cumberly has pointed out that the fascinating thing about the Flower Formula is that its principle can be carried even further than was proposed at the Pushcart Peace Conference. For example, says Professor Cumberly:

If: There are only ¼ as many trucks, traffic will be only ¼ as bad (that is to say, 4 times faster), and you will get 4 loads of potatoes for the price of one.

Or: If there are only ¹⁄₁₀ as many trucks, traffic will be 10 times as fast.

Or: If there are only ¹⁄₁₀₀ as many trucks, traffic will be 100 times as fast, etc.

One could, in fact, Professor Cumberly says jokingly, one could keep on reducing the number of trucks almost indefinitely without hurting business at all.

Counting Numbers in Sequence

The teacher in *Math Curse*, Mrs. Fibonacci, asks the students for examples of counting patterns. If we follow the sequence in the first set—1, 2, 3, 4, 5, 6, 7, 8, 9, 10—the next numbers would be 11, 12, 13. If we follow the sequence in the second set—2, 4, 6, 8, 10—the next numbers would be 12, 14, 16.

1. The following patterns are more difficult. Find the pattern and list the next three numbers that follow in the sequence.

   a. 1, 2, 4, 7, 11, … [16, 22, 29]

   b. 1, 2, 5, 10, 17, … [26, 37, 50]

   c. 1, 4, 9, 16, 25, … [36, 49, 64 if the student sees the pattern as $1^2, 2^2, 3^2, 4^2, …$; or 33, 46, 64 if the student sees the pattern as add 3, add 5, add 7, add 9…]

   d. 4, 7, 13, 22, 34, … [49, 67, 88]

The Fibonacci Numbers

Mrs. Fibonacci says, "I always count 1, 1, 2, 3, 5, 8, 13 …" Can you figure out her pattern? What are the next three numbers in the sequence? [21, 34, 55; The pattern is to add each number to the one that comes before it to get the next number—$1 + 1 = 2; 1 + 2 = 3; 2 + 3 = 5$; $3 + 5 = 8; 5 + 8 = 13$ … continuing forever.]

Historically, this sequence was derived by the Italian mathematician Leonardo Fibonacci in 1202. The sequence is called *recursive* because it repeats itself over and over again. The Fibonacci numbers are so important to mathematicians that an entire magazine is published exclusively on this subject four times a year—the *Fibonacci Quarterly*.

Work Figure 1.3 on page 16 together as a class, in small groups, or as individual assignments.

Answers to Figure 1.3

1. Sum of the Numbers

	Calculated Sum	Pattern
$1 + 1 + 2 + 3$	= 7	= $8 - 1$
$1 + 1 + 2 + 3 + 5$	= 12	= $13 - 1$
$1 + 1 + 2 + 3 + 5 + 8$	= 20	= $21 - 1$

2. Sum of the Squares

	Calculated Sum	Pattern
$1^2 + 1^2 + 2^2 + 3^2 + 5^2$	= 40	= 5×8
$1^2 + 1^2 + 2^2 + 3^2 + 5^2 + 8^2$	= 104	= 8×13
$1^2 + 1^2 + 2^2 + 3^2 + 5^2 + 8^2 + 13^2$	= 273	= 13×21

Figure 1.3 Reproducible
Patterns in Fibonacci Sums and Squares

1. Find the sum of the first six consecutive Fibonacci numbers. What is the pattern? Follow this model:

Sum of the Numbers	Calculated Sum	Pattern
1	= 1	= 2 − 1
1 + 1	= 2	= 3 − 1
1 + 1 + 2	= 4	= 5 − 1
1 + 1 + 2 + 3	= _____	= _____
1 + 1 + 2 + 3 + 5	= _____	= _____
1 + 1 + 2 + 3 + 5 + 8	= _____	= _____

2. Find the sum of the squares of the first seven Fibonacci numbers. What is the pattern? Follow this model:

Sum of the Squares	Calculated Sum	Pattern
1^2	= 1	= 1×1
$1^2 + 1^2$	= 2	= 2×2
$1^2 + 1^2 + 2^2$	= 6	= 2×3
$1^2 + 1^2 + 2^2 + 3^2$	= 15	= 3×5
$1^2 + 1^2 + 2^2 + 3^2 + 5^2$	= 40	= _____
_____	= _____	= _____
_____	= _____	= _____

3. Continue the Fibonacci sequence for twenty numbers.

4. Make ratios of each two successive Fibonacci numbers.

5. Convert the ratios to decimals and round to the nearest thousandth. (A calculator would be helpful.)

6. When did you feel like you did not need to calculate more conversions? Did you stop and go to the end of the list to see if it followed the pattern? What is the pattern?

7. Try one more. Does your prediction hold true? $\dfrac{121,393}{75,025}$

3. 1, 1, 2, 3, 5, 8, 13, 21, 34, 55, 89, 144, 233, 377, 610, 987, 1597, 2584, 4181, 6765

4. $\frac{1}{1}, \frac{2}{1}, \frac{3}{2}, \frac{5}{3}, \frac{8}{5}, \frac{13}{8}, \frac{21}{13}, \frac{34}{21}, \frac{55}{34}, \frac{89}{55}, \frac{144}{89}, \frac{233}{144}, \frac{377}{233}, \frac{610}{377}, \frac{987}{610}, \frac{1597}{987}, \frac{2584}{1597}, \frac{4181}{2584}, \frac{6765}{4181}$

5. 1.000, 2.000, 1.500, 1.667, 1.600, 1.625, 1.615, 1.619, 1.618, 1.618, 1.618, 1.618, 1.618, 1.618, 1.618, 1.618, 1.618

6. Ratios of consecutive Fibonacci numbers will continue to be close to 1.618.

7. 1.618; yes

Pascal's Triangle Pattern

Another special number pattern is Pascal's Triangle. Blaise Pascal was a math genius who lived during the 1600s in France, 400 years after Fibonacci. Make a copy of Figure 1.4 on page 19, Pascal's Triangle, for each student.

1. Study Pascal's Triangle and list all the patterns you can find.

[Sample answers: (1) Each row is symmetrical. (2) Each diagonal is repeated on the opposite side.]

2. Have students draw in diagonal connecting lines like this:

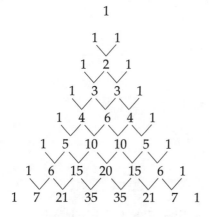

What is the pattern?   [The lower number is the sum of the two above it.]

3. Find the sum of the numbers across each row.   [row 1 = 1, row 2 = 2, row 3 = 4, row 4 = 8, row 5 = 16, row 6 = 32, row 7 = 64, row 8 = 128] What is the pattern?   [Each row is two times the sum of the previous row, or each row is a power of 2: 2^0(1), 2^1(2), 2^2 (2 × 2), 2^3 (2 × 2 × 2), 2^4 (2 × 2 × 2 × 2), 2^5 (2 × 2 × 2 × 2 × 2) ...]

4. Powers of two sound like they would be a small amount; however, their increase is dramatic. To help students visualize the increase, have them fold a piece of paper of any size in half, in half again, and so on, each fold doubling the number of layers of the last fold. Before they actually begin, let the students estimate how many folds they think they will be able to make. How many thicknesses will the paper be after each fold?   [one fold: 1 × 2 = 2; two folds: 2 × 2 = 4; three folds: 4 × 2 = 8; continue recording each fold]

Have students guess how thick the paper would be after fifty folds. For a humorous account of this activity, read the chapter entitled "Corkers" in Roald Dahl's autobiography, *Boy* (1984).

5. In each diagonal, what is the sum of the numbers? [1, 1, 2, 3, 5, 8, 13, 21]

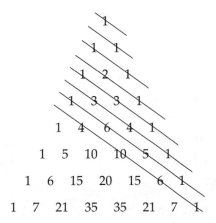

6. What are these numbers called? [the Fibonacci sequence]

7. Add four more rows to the triangle.

Answer

```
         1   8   28   56   70   56   28   8   1
       1   9   36   84  126  126   84  36   9   1
     1  10  45  120  210  252  210  120  45  10   1
   1  11  55  165  330  462  462  330  165  55  11   1
```

Counting in Base 4

Humans have ten fingers and ten numerals: 0, 1, 2, 3, 4, 5, 6, 7, 8, 9. This is a base-ten system of counting. To continue counting after we have reached our highest numeral, 9, we put a 1 in the ten's place and a 0 in the one's place—10.

On the planet Tetra, people have four fingers. (*Tetra* means "four.") They have only four numerals: 0, 1, 2, 3. After Tetrans have reached their highest numeral, 3, they put a 1 in the four's place and a 0 in the one's place. So four is represented as 10_4. Here is the Tetran system of counting compared to base ten.

Base 10	1	2	3	4	5	6	7	8	9	10	11	12	13	14	15	16
Base 4	1	2	3	10	11	12	13	20	21	22	23	30	31	32	33	

1. We use the subscript 4 to remind us that we are in base four. Five is 11_4, six is 12_4, seven is 13_4. What is eight? [20_4]

Figure 1.4 Reproducible
Pascal's Triangle

```
                    1
                 1     1
              1     2     1
           1     3     3     1
        1     4     6     4     1
      1    5    10    10    5    1
    1    6    15   20   15    6    1
  1   7   21   35   35   21   7   1
```

2. The number 33_4 has a 3 in the four's place and a 3 in the one's place. In expanded notation we would write: $(3 \times 4) + (3 \times 1) = 12 + 3 = 15$.

    a. In Tetra what number follows 33?   [100]

    b. How is that written in expanded notation?   [$(1 \times 16) + (0 \times 4) + (0 \times 1) =$ 16 + 0 + 0 = 16. Each place is a power of four—one (4^0), four (4^1), sixteen (4^2), sixty-four (4^3), and so on.]

3. Make a chart that continues to compare base ten to base four (Tetran) up to 26_{10}.

    Answer

Base 10	17	18	19	20	21	22	23	24	25	26
Base 4	101	102	103	110	111	112	113	120	121	122

Counting in Base 2

On the planet Binary, which means "having to do with the number two," people have two fingers and two numerals, 0 and 1. Their place values are all powers of two: one's, two's, four's, eight's, sixteen's, and so forth. Written with exponents, they are: $2^0, 2^1, 2^2, 2^3, 2^4, \ldots$. This is how their counting system compares to the base ten system.

Base 10	1	2	3	4	5	6	7	8
Base 2	1	10	11	100	101	110	111	1000

1. How do Binarians write nine?   [1001]   In expanded notation it is written:

$$(1 \times 2^3) + (0 \times 2^2) + (0 \times 2^1) + (1 \times 2^0) = (1 \times 8) + (0 \times 4) + (0 \times 2) + (0 \times 1)$$
$$= 8 + 0 + 0 + 1$$
$$= 9$$

2. Write your age in the binary system and also in expanded notation to prove your answer.

    Answers for various ages

    $10_{10} = 1010_2$
    $(1 \times 2^3) + (0 \times 2^2) + (1 \times 2^1) + (0 \times 2^0) = (1 \times 8) + (0 \times 4) + (1 \times 2) + (0 \times 1)$
    $= 8 + 0 + 2 + 0 = 10$

    $11_{10} = 1011_2$
    $(1 \times 2^3) + (0 \times 2^2) + (1 \times 2^1) + (1 \times 2^0) = (1 \times 8) + (0 \times 4) + (1 \times 2) + (1 \times 1)$
    $= 8 + 0 + 2 + 1 = 11$

$12_{10} = 1100_2$

$(1 \times 2^3) + (1 \times 2^2) + (0 \times 2^1) + (0 \times 2^0) = 8 + 4 + 0 + 0 = 12$

$13_{10} = 1101_2$

$(1 \times 2^3) + (1 \times 2^2) + (0 \times 2^1) = (1 \times 2^0) = 8 + 4 + 0 + 1 = 13$

$14_{10} = 1110_2$

$(1 \times 2^3) + (1 \times 2^2) + (1 \times 2^1) + (0 \times 2^0) = 8 + 4 + 2 + 0 = 14$

$15_{10} = 1111_2$

$(1 \times 2^3) + (1 \times 2^2) + (1 \times 2^1) + (1 \times 2^0) = 8 + 4 + 2 + 1 = 15$

3. Convert these base ten numbers to the binary system: 7, 16, 23, 38.

   $[111_2, 10000_2, 10111_2, 100110_2]$

4. Convert these binary numbers to base ten: 10101010_2, 10001011_2, 1101100_2.

   [170, 139, 108]

5. The cover of the MCMXCV edition of the book *Math Curse* lists the book's price as $16.99. Then the price is listed as $1001 BINARY. Is this close enough to $16.99 to be a good equivalent? What is right or wrong with the price?

   Answer

   $16.99 is almost $17.00. A binary price of $1001 is equal to $9.00. The amount $17.00 would be written as $10,001. It can be proven in expanded notation:

   $$(1 \times 2^4) + (0 \times 2^3) + (0 \times 2^2) + (0 \times 2^1) + (1 \times 2^0) = (1 \times 16) + (0 \times 8) + (0 \times 4) + (0 \times 2) + (1 \times 1)$$
   $$= 16 + 0 + 0 + 0 + 1 = 17$$

Counting in Base 8

Some computers work by using a binary system, but some computer programmers use a base-eight system.

1. What digits can base-eight programmers use?   [0, 1, 2, 3, 4, 5, 6, 7]

2. What are base-eight place values expressed in exponential form? $[8^0, 8^1, 8^2, 8^3, 8^4, ...]$

3. What are the place values' base-ten equivalents?   [1, 8, 64, 512, 4096, ...]

4. Write these base-ten numbers in base eight: 18, 305, 620, and 5192. Prove their values by using expanded notation.

   Answers

   $18_{10} = 22_8$

   $22_8 = (2 \times 8^1) + (2 \times 8^0)$

   $\quad = (2 \times 8) + (2 \times 1) = 16 + 2 = 18_{10}$

$$305_{10} = 461_8$$
$$461_8 = (4 \times 8^2) + (6 \times 8^1) + (1 \times 80)$$
$$= (4 \times 64) + (6 \times 8) + (1 \times 1) = 256 + 48 + 1 = 305_{10}$$

$$620_{10} = 1154_8$$
$$1154_8 = (1 \times 8^3) + (1 \times 8^2) + (5 \times 8^1) + (4 \times 8^0)$$
$$= (1 \times 512) + (1 \times 64) + (5 \times 8) + (4 \times 1) = 512 + 64 + 40 + 4 = 620_{10}$$

$$5192_{10} = 12110_8$$
$$12110_8 = (1 \times 8^4) + (2 \times 8^3) + (1 \times 8^2) + (1 \times 8^1) + (0 \times 8^0)$$
$$= (1 \times 4096) + (2 \times 512) + (1 \times 64) + (1 \times 8) + (0 \times 1)$$
$$= 4096 + 1024 + 64 + 8 + 0 = 5192_{10}$$

Solving Problems without Fractions

The math lunatic solves the dividing-the-cupcakes problem in a way that does not involve fractions. What practical ways can you use to solve the following problems without using fractions?

1.   A pizza is cut into fourths. Melissa will cut it in smaller pieces so five people can share the pizza equally. Into how many pieces does she have to cut it?
     [Sample answer: Give four people the pieces that have already been cut and ask each of them to give the other person an equal share.]

2.   Rosa drove $25\frac{2}{3}$ miles from her house to the mall. On the way home she stopped at Tony's, which is $5\frac{1}{2}$ miles from her house. How far is it from Tony's house to the mall?   [Sample answer: Round $25\frac{2}{3}$ miles to 26. Round $5\frac{1}{2}$ miles to 6 then subtract: $26 - 6 = 20$ miles. The exact answer is $20\frac{1}{6}$ miles, but who cares about $\frac{1}{6}$ mile when you're going to the mall?]

Note Aren't these really the ways we use math in everyday situations?

Venn Diagrams

On the copies of *Math Curse* that have book jackets, a Venn diagram visually illustrates which books Scieszka and Smith have written together. Venn diagrams can show that separate groups have something in common or nothing in common.

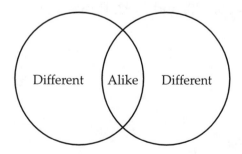

1. Draw a Venn diagram for the following statement:
    Some birds are tame. (B = {birds}; T = {tame animals})

2. Draw the Venn Diagram:
    No giraffe wears kneepads. (G = {giraffes}; K = {kneepad wearers})

3. Draw the Venn Diagram:
    Some fruits are speckled. (F = {fruits}; S = {speckled things})

    Answers

    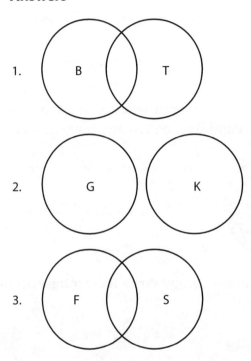

4. Write a statement that would fit the following diagram:

    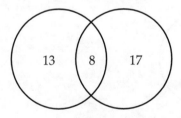

    [Sample answer: In a physical education class, thirteen students would like to play soccer and seventeen students would like to play volleyball. Eight students want to play both.]

Writing and Drawing Venn Diagrams

A Venn diagram can show the intersection and the union of two sets. The intersection of two sets is the set of elements found in both sets. For intersection of sets the ∩ symbol is used. This is how the intersection of sets A and B is written and diagrammed.

A = {2, 4, 6, 8, 10}
B = {4, 8, 12, 16}
A∩B = {4, 8}

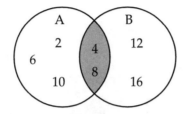

The union of two sets is the set of all the elements in both sets. For union of sets the ∪ symbol is used. This is how the union of sets A and B is written and diagrammed.

A = {2, 4, 6, 8, 10}
B = {4, 8, 12, 16}
A∪B = {2, 4, 6, 8, 10, 12, 16}

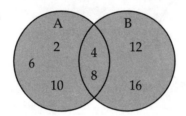

Draw Venn diagrams for the pairs of sets listed below. Write their intersections and unions in complete mathematical statements.

1. R = {0, 1, 2, 3, 4}
S = {−4, −3, −2, −1, 0}

Answer

R∩S = {0}
R∪S = {−4, −3, −2, −1, 0, 1, 2, 3, 4}

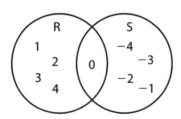

2. L = {-3, −2, −1, 0, 1}
M = {−2, −1, 0, 1, 2}

Answer

L∩M = {−2, −1, 0, 1}
L∪M = {−3, −2, −1, 0, 1, 2}

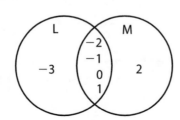

Related Books

Dahl, Roald. *Boy.* New York: Farrar, Straus, & Giroux, 1984.

Merrill, Jean. *The Pushcart War.* New York: HarperCollins Publishers, 1992.

Paulos, John Allen. *A Mathematician Reads the Newspaper.* New York: Anchor Books, 1995.

Perl, Teri. *Biographies of Women Mathematicians Plus Related Activities.* Menlo Park, California: Addison Wesley Publishing, 1978.

Perl, Teri. *Women and Numbers: Lives of Women Mathematicians Plus Discovery Activities.* San Carlos, California: World Publishing/Tetra, 1993.

Reimer, Luetta and Wilbert Reimer. *Mathematicians Are People, Too: Stories from the Lives of Great Mathematicians, Book 1.* Palo Alto, California: Seymour Publications, 1990.

Reimer, Luetta and Wilbert Reimer. *Mathematicians Are People, Too: Stories from the Lives of Great Mathematicians, Book 2.* Palo Alto, California: Seymour Publications, 1994.

White, Laurence B. and Ray Broekel. *Math-a-Magic: Number Tricks for Magicians.* Niles, Illinois: Albert Whitman & Company, 1990.

The Man Who Counted:
A Collection of Mathematical Adventures

by Malba Tahan
New York: W. W. Norton and Company, 1993

In this tale, Beremiz Samir, a Persian mathematician who lived in the thirteenth century, travels on exotic journeys. In each chapter he solves a mathematical problem, gives wise advice, or settles a dispute. Every chapter contains a math problem. Go through the book to work and discuss the stated problem or extend the concept with activities such as those following. Although the book is written for adults, it is appropriate to read aloud to intermediate and middle school students.

Topic Number sense in culture

Objectives To develop and apply a variety of strategies to solve problems

Applicable NCTM Standards 1, 2, 3, 4, 5, 6, 7, 8, 12

Counting with Beremiz Samir

The man who counts, Beremiz Samir, is so good at counting that he can correctly calculate the number of things at a glance. His travelling companion, Hanak Tade Maia, thinks Beremiz should get a job with the government to "count populations, armies, and flocks … the resources of the country, the value of its harvest, its taxes, its commodities, all the wealth of the state" (page 9).

1. List ten things that you would count in order to benefit government, business, or society if you had this gift.

2. What are some quick ways to count or to estimate the number of things?

    Sample answers

    (1) Count things in an array (for instance, window panes in an office building or members of a marching band), by counting the number down and the number across and multiplying:

    XXXXXXXXXXXX
    XXXXXXXXXXXX $12 \times 3 = 36$
    XXXXXXXXXXXX

    (2) To estimate a group (for example, a large crowd or a flock), imagine a 100s grid covering the group. Count the number in what you consider to be one square and multiply that by 100.

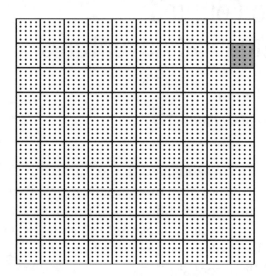

$20 \times 100 = 2000$

Faulty Reasoning

1. Find the faulty reasoning in the camel inheritance problem in Chapter 3, "Beasts of Burden," and show mathematical work explaining the situation.

Answer

The father made a mistake when he thought he could divide his herd of thirty-five camels among his sons by giving one son half the herd, one son a third of the herd, and one son a ninth of the herd. This calculation does not total the whole herd: $1/2 + 1/3 + 1/9 = 17/18$; $17/18$ is less than a whole herd. According to the father's wishes, this is how the division would have been calculated:

$1/2$ of 35 = $17\frac{1}{2}$ camels
$1/3$ of 35 = $11\frac{2}{3}$ camels
$1/9$ of 35 = $3\frac{8}{9}$ camels
Total: $33\frac{1}{18}$ camels (not 35)

With this calculation, $1\frac{7}{18}$ (almost two) camels would not have been willed to anyone. Beremiz recognized this and knew that if he offered to include his own camel in the herd before dividing it, the two whole camels would be unaccounted for in the end. Then Beremiz claimed the two leftover unwilled camels for himself.

$1/2$ of 36 = 18
$1/3$ of 36 = 12
$1/9$ of 36 = 4
Total: 34 camels

Calculating Speaking Rate

1. In Chapter 5, Beremiz calculates his speaking rate at 36 words per minute.

    a. Show the steps for how this can be calculated.   [Time = 24 hours × 60 minutes × 8 days = 11,520 minutes; total number of words spoken = 414,720; words per minute = 414,720 ÷ 11,520 = 36]

    b. Is this an accurate estimate?   [No. He did not speak continuously for all 11,520 minutes—8 days—without stopping.]

2. If Beremiz slept 8 hours a day, how many words per minute did he speak?
    [24 hours − 8 hours (sleeping) = 16 hours
    16 hours × 60 minutes × 8 days = 7680 minutes
    Number of words = 414,720
    Words per minute = 414,720 ÷ 7680 = 54]

Calculating Lodging Costs

Can we simplify the cost of lodging problem on pages 23–26? Try the following ideas:

1. A jeweler promises to pay 20 dinars for lodging if he sells his jewels for 100 dinars. He promises to pay 35 dinars for lodging if he sells his jewels for 200

dinars. Since he sells the jewels for 140 dinars, about halfway between 100 and 200, couldn't he offer to pay the innkeeper an amount about halfway between 20 and 35 dinars? What would you offer the innkeeper?   [27½ dinars is between 20 and 35; it is the median amount. Would you offer him less—perhaps 26 dinars—because 140 is less than halfway between 100 and 200?]

2.   Work the problem again, this time using the ratio of lodging price to jewelry price to find what percentage of income he has promised to pay the innkeeper for his lodging. Now how much should the jeweler pay?   [A fair amount to pay the innkeeper would be 26¼ dinars. He could offer to pay him 26 dinars, of course, since there was no firm price.]

   a.   Calculate the percentage of sales he would pay for lodging if he sold the jewels for 100 dinars.   [$^{20}/_{100}$ = 20%]

   b.   Calculate the percentage of sales that he would pay for lodging if he sold the jewels for 200 dinars.   [$^{35}/_{200}$ = 17.5%]

   c.   Find the median percentage.   [18.75% because (17.5% + 20%)/2 = 18.75%]

   d.   Use the median percentage to find what the jeweler should pay for lodging after selling the jewels for 140 dinars.   [18.75% of 140 = 26.25 dinars because 18.75% × 140 = .1875 × 140 = 26.25]

Writing Equivalents

Look at the Four Fours problem on pages 38–41 of *The Man Who Counted*.

1.   It is possible to write equivalents of the numbers 0–10, each time using four fours. Can this be done with four of any other number? If so, demonstrate.

2.   It is possible to write the numbers 0–50 using six fives. How many can you come up with? You can use any operation or symbol you know. Don't forget square roots and decimals.

Examples

$$1 = \frac{555}{555}$$

$$2 = .5 - .5 + \frac{5}{5} + \frac{5}{5}$$

$$3 = \frac{5}{5} + \frac{5}{5} + \frac{5}{5}$$

$$4 = \frac{5 \times 5}{5} - \frac{\sqrt{5} \times \sqrt{5}}{5}$$

$$10 = 5.5 + 5.5 - \frac{5}{5}$$

$$18 = (5 \times 5) - \left(5 + \frac{5+5}{5}\right)$$

$$24 = \frac{5 \times 5 \times 5}{5} - \frac{5}{5}$$

$$49 = (5 \times 5) + (5 \times 5) - \frac{5}{5}$$

Perfect Numbers

Beremiz explains on page 64 that a perfect number is "one that is equal to the sum of its divisors [factors] excluding the number itself." See the examples of the perfect numbers 28 and 6 on pages 64 and 65. Prove that 496 is a perfect number. [Divisors: 1, 2, 4, 8, 16, 31, 62, 124, 248; Sum of divisors: 1 + 2 + 4 + 8 +16 + 31 + 62 + 124 + 248 = 496]

Mathematical Terms

In Beremiz's first mathematics lesson to Telassim, the sheik's daughter, he gives brief explanations for the following terms (pages 73–74):

- number

- measurement

- mathematics

- arithmetic

- algebra

- geometry

1. After thinking about what Beremiz says, read more about these subjects. An encyclopedia will be useful. Then write a short paragraph about each concept, explaining what it is and why we need it.

2. The mathematician states that "[m]athematics ... is the basis of all the arts and sciences" (page 74). Write an explanation of how you think mathematics plays a part in painting, music, sculpture, and architecture.

Magic Squares

Magic squares are shown on pages 103 and 104 of *The Man Who Counted*. In a magic square, the sum of the numbers in every row, column, and diagonal must be the same. Make a copy of Figure 1.5 for every student.

1.   Fill in the missing numbers on the square using multiples of 3.

2.   Fill in the squares using integers so that each row, column, and diagonal equals 0.

3.   Fill in the squares so that the sum of every row, column, and diagonal is 3⁹⁄₁₆.

Answers

1.

12	27	6
9	15	21
24	3	18

2.

−5	−7	12
17	0	−17
−12	7	5

3.

$1\frac{1}{8}$	$1\frac{1}{16}$	$1\frac{3}{8}$
$1\frac{7}{16}$	$1\frac{3}{16}$	$\frac{15}{16}$
1	$1\frac{5}{16}$	$1\frac{1}{4}$

Pythagorean Theorem

Beremiz explains the Pythagorean theorem: for a right triangle, $a^2 + b^2 = c^2$, or "the area of a square drawn on the hypotenuse is equal to the sum of the squares drawn on the adjacent sides" (page 131). The illustration on page 132 proves that for a right triangle with sides of 3, 4, and 5, that $3^2 + 4^2 = 5^2$, or $9 + 16 = 25$.

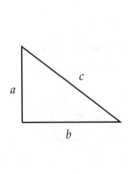

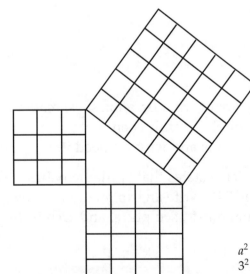

$a = 3$
$b = 4$
$c = 5$

$a^2 + b^2 = c^2$
$3^2 + 4^2 = 5^2$
$9 + 16 = 25$

Figure 1.5 Reproducible
Magic Squares

1. Fill in the squares with multiples of three so that every row, column, and diagonal adds up to the same sum.

12		
	15	
	3	18

2. Fill in the squares with integers so that every row, column, and diagonal equals 0.

−5		
17	0	

3. Fill in the squares so that the sum of every row, column, and diagonal is $3\frac{9}{16}$.

		$\frac{15}{16}$
1	$1\frac{5}{16}$	

1. Hand out copies of Figure 1.6 to the students. Using the illustration on page 132 as a model, cut out appropriate squares of grid paper to create a similar proof for a right triangle with sides measuring 5, 12, and 13. If the number of grid squares of the sides can completely cover the grid squares of the hypotenuse, the proof is correct.

    Answer

    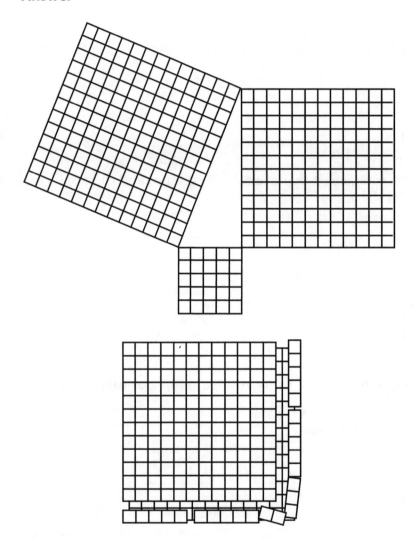

2. Write the Pythagorean theorem statements for a right triangle with sides of 39, 36, and 15.

    Answer

    $$a^2 + b^2 = c^2$$
    $$15^2 + 36^2 = 39^2$$
    $$225 + 1296 = 1521$$

Figure 1.6 Reproducible   Grid Paper

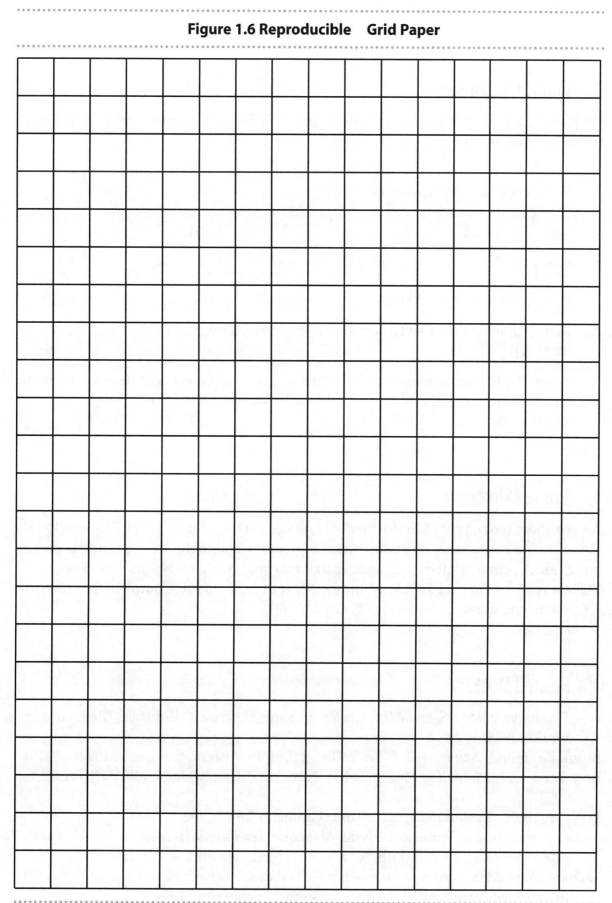

Counting Systems

On page 151 Beremiz explains various counting systems. (See pages 18–22 of this text for more work in different base systems.)

1. Compare counting in our decimal (base-ten) system with the quinary system. Use a chart to show counting to 12_{10}.

Base 10	1	2	3	4	5	6	7	8	9	10	11	12
Base 5	1	2	3	4	10	11	12	13	14	20	21	22

   Do you see a pattern that is easy to recognize?   [$5_{10} = 10_5, 10_{10} = 20_5, 15_{10} = 30_5, ...$]

2. In the Chaldean base-sixty system, how would you write: 17, 128, and 182? [17, 28, 32]

3. Count the following number tally marks and write the answer in decimal, quinary, and Roman numerals: ‖‖‖ ‖‖‖ ‖‖‖ ‖‖‖ ‖‖‖ ‖‖‖ ‖‖‖ ‖‖‖ | | | [43, 133_5, XLIII]

Prime Numbers

A very short biography of Eratosthenes is related on pages 200–201 of *The Man Who Counted*. The name Sieve of Eratosthenes is given to a table that we use to find prime numbers. A prime number is a number that has only two factors—itself and one. Make a copy of Figure 1.7, Prime Numbers, for every student. Complete the sieve to find the prime numbers between 1 and 100.

Related Books

Ary, Daniel W. *Middle School Math Challenge.* Santa Barbara, California: The Learning Works, 1995.

Blum, Raymond. *Mathemagic.* New York: Sterling Publishing Company, 1992.

Bolt, Brian. *A Mathematical Pandora's Box.* New York: Cambridge University Press, 1993.

Bushnaq, Iner. *Arab Folktales.* New York: Pantheon Books, 1986.

Hyde, Arthur A. and Pamela R. Hyde. *Mathwise: Teaching Mathematical Thinking and Problem Solving.* Portsmouth, New Hampshire: Heinemann, 1991.

Sachar, Louis. *More Sideways Arithmetics From Wayside School: More Than 50 Brainteasing Puzzles.* New York: An Apple Paperback, Scholastic, 1994.

Figure 1.7 Reproducible
Prime Numbers

Directions Cross out 1 because it is not prime. Circle 2 and cross out all multiples of 2 to 100. Circle 3 and cross all multiples of 3 to 100. Continue this process for 5 and 7. Circle the numbers which have not been crossed out. These are the prime numbers between 1 and 100.

Sieve of Eratosthenes

1	2	3	4	5	6	7	8	9	10
11	12	13	14	15	16	17	18	19	20
21	22	23	24	25	26	27	28	29	30
31	32	33	34	35	36	37	38	39	40
41	42	43	44	45	46	47	48	49	50
51	52	53	54	55	56	57	58	59	60
61	62	63	64	65	66	67	68	69	70
71	72	73	74	75	76	77	78	79	80
81	82	83	84	85	86	87	88	89	90
91	92	93	94	95	96	97	98	99	100

The Phantom Tollbooth

by Norton Juster
New York: Bullseye Books, 1989

Milo is bored with everything until a tollbooth mysteriously appears in his bedroom. When he drives through it, he finds an astonishing realm. Many of his adventures relate to mathematics.

This book touches on many aspects of mathematics curriculum. Different portions of the book can be used while studying such topics as statistics, geometry, or measurement. Because this book is a rich resource, it will also be used as a means to introduce the use of literature to meet language arts objectives. While lessons in this book can be used in either language arts or mathematics class (sometimes even in social studies, science, or art), it is useful as a means to teach students how to view learning and life as an integrated whole—not in compartmentalized and isolated blocks.

If multiple copies of *The Phantom Tollbooth* are available, it can be read and discussed as you would do with any group novel. If not, you can read the book aloud to the students. Some teachers may prefer to read aloud only the portions that will be dealt with in the following lessons. Page numbers are noted.

This book is rich in words, word meanings, connotations, ambiguities, and figures of speech. These can be covered in minilessons as they appear in the book.

Topics A variety of lessons for language arts and mathematics

Objective To begin integrating curricula and incorporating novels into mathematics

Applicable NCTM Standards 1, 2, 3, 4, 5, 6, 7, 10, 13

Language Arts: Synonyms

Milo reads Ordinance 175389-J from the rulebook (page 24). "It shall be unlawful, illegal, and unethical to think, think about thinking, surmise, presume, reason, meditate, or speculate while in the Doldrums." This statement can begin vocabulary building and skills lessons using the dictionary and thesaurus.

1. Do the words "unlawful," "illegal," and "unethical" all have the same meaning? Are there any shades of difference? When might one word be a better choice over the others?

2. Are there differences among the meaning of the words "think," "surmise," "presume," "reason," "meditate," and "speculate"?

3. In the daily schedule printed on pages 26 and 27, time is allotted to daydream, dawdle, delay, bide time, linger, loiter, put off for tomorrow what they could have done today, loaf, lounge, dillydally, waste time, brood, lag, plod, and procrastinate. Choose four of these verbs and write a sentence for each illustrating the various shades of meaning.

4. A dictionary may list a few synonyms for a word's meaning. A thesaurus may list numerous variations. However, a good writer's job is to choose the word that fits best.

   a. These synonyms are on page 38: greetings, salutations, welcome, good afternoon, and hello. Give an example for each that shows it is the best fit or that it is more appropriate in a different circumstance.

   b. Do the same for these synonyms: kingdom, nation, state, commonwealth, realm, empire, palatinate, and principality (pages 38–39).

   c. Does it matter which of the synonyms in part b is used when writing about an area that is ruled? Why?

   d. Why might a writer choose the word "palatinate"?   [It should be used if the writer is describing the territory ruled by a medieval vassal lord. If the writer is just showing off a large vocabulary or thesaurus skills, it is inappropriate.]

   e. Ask the same kind of questions for other examples:

      • of course, certainly, precisely, exactly (page 39)

      • nonsense, ridiculous, fantastic, absurd (page 40)

      • don't need it, no use for it, superfluous, unnecessary, uncalled for (page 79)

      • vehicle, conveyance, rig, charabanc, chariot, buggy, coach, brougham, shandryman (page 79)

5. When might a writer choose a less common synonym?   [Sample answers: When writing about a specific time period, locale, or to paint a more vivid image.]

Can the Worlds of Language and Math Meet?

Chapter 9 begins: "Soon all traces of Dictionopolis had vanished in the distance and all those strange and unknown lands that lay between the kingdoms of word and the kingdom of numbers stretched before them."

1.   Are the kingdoms of words and numbers separate? Why?

2.   Why do we need language for math? How are the two inseparable?

Math Connections: Making Sense

On page 108, Milo has "comparable size" explained to him: A bucket of water could look like an ocean to an ant. It could look like a drink to an elephant. It could look like home to a fish. "So, you see, the way you see things depends a great deal on where you look at them from." Read pages 110–114 about the giant, the midget, the fat man, and the thin man. Milo thinks they are all the same person.

1.   How can this be?   [Sizes and measurement have meaning only when they are comparisons. Big compared to what? Small compared to what?]

2.   How does this compare to Gulliver's Travels?   [In Lilliput, Gulliver is a giant although his own size never changes. In Brobdingnag, the natives are the giants.]

3.   Have students create comparisons of different objects from different perspectives.

4.   We develop number sense by comparison. Have students create statements using this form: _____ could not be the number of _____ , but it could be the number of _____ . Have them do this for small numbers, medium numbers, and large numbers. Do not specify which are small, medium, and large. You will be able to assess their number sense by their choices. Students can work in pairs and illustrate their statements on newsprint. These make colorful, interesting, and sometimes amusing wall displays.

Examples

- 100 could not be the number of kids in this class, but it could be the number of keys on a piano.

- 5000 could not be the number of houses on a block, but it could be the number of shreds of cabbage in coleslaw.

- 1,000,000,000 could not be the number of books in our library, but it could be the number of people in China.

Making Sense of Answers

This road sign appears on page 171:

```
              DIGITOPOLIS

            5  Miles

         1600  Rods

         8800  Yards

       26,400  Feet

      316,800  Inches

      633,600  Half Inches

      AND THEN SOME
```

Humbug wants to travel by miles because it's shorter, and Milo wants to travel by inches because it's quicker (page 171).

1. Do their answers make sense? Where is their reasoning faulty?

2. Students can create similar equivalency charts for other measures and weights. Have them describe when using each measure is appropriate.

    Examples

    •   To remove a wart, a doctor might cut millimeters;

    •   To remove an appendix, she might cut centimeters;

    •   To perform an open-heart surgery, she might cut decimeters.

3. Students should always follow up their problem solving with the question, Does this make sense?

4. Read the story problem which appears on page 174. It goes on and on. As soon as he has hears the problem, Humbug shouts out his answer, "Seventeen!" What should he have asked himself first? What might some appropriate answers be?

5. In every subject ask, Does this make sense? For example, a student giving an oral report on a foreign country stated that its average annual rainfall is 1.7 million. Ask, 1.7 million what?

    a.   What values might be appropriate to report annual amounts of rainfall?

    b.   What could the value 1,700,000 (1.7 million) represent?

6. The Mathemagician says he has "four million eight hundred and twenty-seven thousand six hundred and fifty-nine hairs" on his head (page 179). (Incidentally, he has inserted the word "and" incorrectly twice. He should say "four million eight hundred twenty-seven thousand six hundred fifty-nine hairs.")

    a. Is this reasonable? How is this number written with numerals?   [4,827,659]

    b. He also states that there are "eight million two hundred and forty-seven thousand three hundred and twelve threads" in his robe (pages 179–180). (Again, the two "ands" should be omitted.) Is this reasonable? How is this number written?   [8,247,312]

7. Read other large numbers and have the students write them as they hear them. Do not insert the word "and" unless it stands for a decimal. 317.89 is read "three hundred seventeen and eighty-nine hundredths." 317,000,089 is read "three hundred seventeen million eighty-nine."

Infinity

Chapter 15 introduces the concept of infinity. When the Mathemagician asks Milo what he thinks the greatest number is, Milo says it's "nine trillion, nine hundred ninety-nine billion, nine hundred ninety-nine million, nine hundred ninety-nine thousand, nine hundred ninety-nine" (page 190). The Mathemagician tells him to "add one to it. Now add one again. Now add one again. Now add one ..." Milo discovers he can never stop.

When the Mathemagician asks Milo what the smallest number is, he guesses "One one-millionth?" The Mathemagician says, "Now divide it in half. Now divide it in half again. Now divide it in half ... ." Again, the process can go on forever. This may be the first time students ever consider that smallness is also infinite. Initiate a discussion about what is infinite.

Negative Integers

The conversation on page 186 can serve as an introduction to the understanding of adding integers. Read Dodecahedron's series of questions about adding something, adding nothing, and adding less than nothing. He asks, "And suppose you had something and added less than nothing to it. What would you have then?"

Stop reading and ask students for an answer, which should be "Less." Begin a discussion with this probe: Is it possible to add something and wind up with less?

Order of Operations

A multistep computation problem is presented on page 188:

$$4 + 9 - 2 \times 16 + 1 \div 3 \times 6 - 67 + 8 \times 2 - 3 + 26 - 1 \div 34 + 3 \div 7 + 2 - 5 =$$

Milo says the answer is zero and the Mathemagician agrees. If the operations are performed strictly from left to right, this is correct. However, there are rules for the order in which operations are done.

In many areas of life you must perform tasks in a certain order to get the right results. Name some things that must be done in a specific order. What happens if you add the eggs to a cake after it's baked? What happens if an electrician tries to fix a socket before he turns off the electricity?

Mathematicians have agreed on a specific order in which to perform operations to avoid confusion and to ensure that everyone will get the same results from multistep problems. They are:

Step 1 Perform all work in parentheses first.

Step 2 Then multiply and divide from left to right.

Step 3 Finally, add and subtract from left to right.

Step 4 If there are no parentheses, do the multiplication and division before adding and subtracting.

Step 5 Remember PMDAS (pronounced pemdas): Parentheses, Multiplication, Division, Addition, Subtraction

Examples

- $3 + (10 \div 2)$ Do the operation in parentheses first.
  $3 + 5$ Then add.
  8

- $45 - 10 \times 3$ Multiply first.
  $45 - 30$ Then subtract.
  15

- $7 + 4 \times 3 - 6$ Multiply.
  $7 + 12 - 6$ Add.
  $19 - 6$ Subtract.
  13

- $30 - 15 \div 3$ Divide.
  $30 - 5$ Subtract.
  25

Practice

1. $30 \div (3 \times 2)$ [5]

2. $40 - 15 \div 3$ [35]

3. $7 + 6 \times 3$ [25]

Have students solve the following exercises as written. Then have them remove the parentheses and use the rules for order of operations.

4. $(11 \times 3) - (5 \times 3)$ [18; 18]

5. $(10 + 2) \times (5 - 3)$ [24; 17]

6. $(8 - 2) \times (4 + 3)$ [42; 3]

7. $(8 + 8) \div (4 \times 2)$ [2; 12]

8.   **Here's a challenge!** Have students choose one (or more) practice problem above and create a story problem to fit the operations. Then have them illustrate the solution with a simple drawing.

Example

Using practice problem 4 above, $(11 \times 3) - (5 \times 3)$: In a classroom, have students sit at eleven tables in groups of three. All the students at the first five tables are excused early. How many students remain?

$11 \times 3 =$

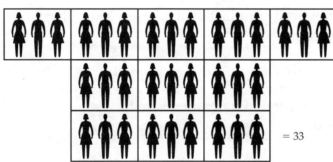

$= 33$

$(11 \times 3) - (5 \times 3) =$

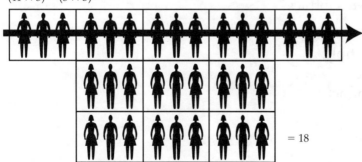

$= 18$

Understanding Averages

Milo meets a partial boy who is .58 of a child (page 195). He is from an average family which has 2.58 children. (Always read decimal fractions as their values. Say "two and fifty-eight hundredths," not "two point five eight.") He is the .58. But he really doesn't mind because the average family also has 1.3 automobiles, and since he is the only one who can drive three-tenths of a car, he gets to use it all the time. "But averages aren't real," objected Milo; "they're just imaginary" (page 196).

1.   What does Milo mean?

2.   What are averages? The partial boy insists we are better off with averages. Read his explanation on page 196 and decide if it is reasonable. Ask your students, "If you have no money and you are with four people who have ten dollars each, on the average, how much does each of you have?"

3.   Brainstorm other situations where averaging does not reflect the situation accurately.

4.   As a class, collect data and find the averages of all the students' children in their families, number of cars, number of televisions, sound equipment (radios, stereos, and CD players) and so on per family. Does anyone fit this profile?

5.   Find a nonsense average.

Example
What is the average birth date of all the class members? List all the birthdays: 6-7-86, 1-28-87, and so forth. Find the average month, the average day, the average year. Before the computation, have students make their best guess of what the date will be and have them explain why. Is there any meaning in this average? Why?

Collecting Data

Milo meets a Senses Taker who needs information before he can take Milo's senses. Look at pages 226–227 to see the questions the Senses Taker asks in collecting his data. Which are reasonable? Which are not? Why?

1.   In the U.S. Population section of *The World Almanac and Book of Facts* (World Almanac Books, yearly), students can discover other information that census takers gather besides population statistics—how many people speak other languages, how many houses have indoor plumbing or air conditioning, how many women work, and so on. Have students create and take their own census surveys using questions such as the those asked by the Census Bureau or the Senses Taker.

2. For what areas can they compute averages (that make sense)?

3. How can the gathered data best be communicated? Pictorials? Charts? Graphs? Tables? Construct and display them.

2

COMPUTATION AND ESTIMATION

How to Get Fabulously Rich

by Thomas Rockwell

New York: Dell Yearling, 1990

Billy buys a lottery ticket and the odds of his winning are one in twelve million. He has strange ways of determining how to choose the winning numbers. Most of Billy's problems have to do with dividing his winnings with people who claim a portion.

Topic Real-life computation, probability

Objective To put ideas and words to computation problems in order to demonstrate understanding

Applicable NCTM Standards 1, 2, 3, 4, 5, 6, 7, 11, 13

Making Sensible Computations

In *How to Get Fabulously Rich*, Tom thinks he may be able to get into *The Guinness Book of Records* by touching his toes a record number of times—5,473,989 times (page 11).

1. How long would it take you to do 5,473,989 toe touches? Explain all the steps you need to go through to solve this problem.   [Sample answer: With a stopwatch, I timed myself to see how long it would take to do 50 toe touches. Since it took 1'15" (1$\frac{1}{4}$ minutes) to do 50, I thought it would take me 2$\frac{1}{2}$ minutes to do 100. Then I figured out how many hundreds in 5,473,989—54,739.89. To make the work easier, I rounded that to 54,740. I multiplied that by 2.5 to figure out how many minutes it would take—54,740 × 2.5 = 136,850 minutes. I divided by 60 to find the number of hours (136,850 ÷ 60 ≈ 2281) and divided that by 24 to find how many days (2281 ÷ 24 ≈ 95 days). That's about 3 months without stopping.

2. Is anything wrong with Tom's idea?   [Nobody can perform an activity for 3 months without stopping. This answer assumes that the person will not tire or slow down.]

3. Does your answer seem to make sense mathematically? How do you know the computation is correct?

4. Did you use pencil and paper or a calculator to do your computation? Why?

Making Sensible Estimates

Another book which discusses world records is *I'm Going to Be Famous* by Tom Birdseye (1986). Arlo and his friends are determined to break four records in *The Guinness Book of Records*. Arlo is going to eat seventeen bananas in less than 2 minutes; Ben is going to eat three whole lemons with the seeds and skin in less than 15.2 seconds; Mike is going to eat 3 pounds, 6 ounces of ice cream (3 quarts) in less than 50 seconds; and Kerry wants to break the melon seed-spitting record of 65 feet, 4 inches. She says, "That's twice the length of Room 11 at Lincoln Elementary School. I'll bet that's as long as 150 hot dogs laid out end to end" (page 81).

1. Explain all the steps involved to see if Kerry's estimate is accurate.

2. Have everyone in the class come up with a different way of describing about how long 65 feet 4 inches is.

3. Arlo eats one banana in 10.4 seconds (page 70). Can he set the record at this rate? Explain the steps you went through to find this answer.

4. A few days before the record-setting day, Arlo believes he can eat three bananas in less than 21 seconds. Can he set the record at this rate? Explain.

5. What are some factors the banana stuffer, the lemon eater, and the ice cream gobbler have not taken into consideration while training?   [Arlo has never checked to see how many bananas his stomach can hold, Ben doesn't think about how all the acid in the lemons will hurt his digestive system, and Mike doesn't realize that eating ice cream so quickly will give him a headache and cause him to pass out.]

6. Kerry's best seed-spit length is 42 feet, $14\frac{3}{4}$ inches. What is strange about this measurement?   [It is not expressed in lowest terms which would be 43 feet, $2\frac{3}{4}$ inches.]

7. How far away from the 65 feet, 4 inch record is she?   [22 feet, $1\frac{1}{4}$ inches]

Writing Word Problems

In Chapter XII of *How to Get Fabulously Rich*, Billy labors over the choice of his lottery numbers and tries to figure out if they are good choices mathematically or magically (page 60–68).

1. Have students choose ten numbers that they might use for lottery numbers. Then they must "explain" their numbers by writing a story problem for each one. Make the constraints or rules for the problems fit whatever kind of computation you have been working on. For instance, you could use these rules:

    *   All problems must have at least four steps.

    *   Five of the "explanations" must include all four operations—adding, subtracting, multiplying, and dividing.

    *   Half of the problems must include negative integers.

    *   One problem must include fractions.

    *   One problem must include decimals.

    Example
    A student chooses lottery numbers 2, 24, 18, 98, 42, 33, 12, 51, 57, 75. Now the student must write a word problem explaining each number choice. The lottery number must be the answer to the problem.

    *   The first number, 2, uses fractions and has four steps:

        Tony's mother gave him three graham crackers which he shared evenly with his brother Mac. When Mac broke his graham crackers along the lines that mark the crackers into fourths, he dropped and stepped on three of them. Tony felt sorry for Mac and gave him half of one of his crackers. Mother didn't see what Mac had done, so she gave Tony three more fourths. How many graham crackers did Tony end up with?

        Step 1 3 ÷ 2 = 1½ crackers each

        Step 2 1½ − ¾ = ¾ cracker

        Step 3 ¾ + ½ (from Tony) = 1¼ crackers

        Step 4 1¼ + ¾ (from Mother) = 2 crackers

        The answer, 2, is the first lottery number.

- The second number, 24, uses four operations and has four steps:

  Nine baseball players each contribute $10 to buy snacks to eat on the bus on the way to a tournament. To speed up the shopping, they split into two groups and divide the money evenly. One group spends $27.32 on sandwiches, $3.40 for peanuts, and $6.46 for soft drinks. The other group spends $11.61 on candy, $9.00 on chips, and $8.21 for juice drinks. How much money does the team have left over?

  Step 1 Total money is $9 \times \$10 = \$90$.

  Each group gets $\$90 \div 2 = \$45$.

  Step 2 One group spends $\$27.32 + \$3.40 + \$6.46 = \$37.18$.

  Other group spends $\$11.61 + \$9.00 + \$8.21 = \$28.82$.

  Step 3 One group's change is $\$45.00 - \$37.18 = \$7.82$.

  Other group's change is $\$45.00 - \$28.82 = \$16.18$.

  Step 4 Total change is $\$7.82 + \$16.18 = \$24.00$.

  The answer, 24, is the second lottery number.

- The third number, 18, uses negative integers and has four steps:

  Amanda had a checkbook balance of $73.00 on Thursday. Friday she wrote three checks: one for $46.91, one for $38.00, and one for $13.62. Monday she deposited $43.53. What is her balance now?

  Step 1 $\$73.00 - \$46.91 = \$26.09$

  Step 2 $\$26.09 - \$38.00 = -\$11.91$

  Step 3 $-\$11.91 - \$13.62 = -\$25.53$

  Step 4 $-\$25.53 + 443.53 = \$18.00$

  The answer, 18, is the third lottery number.

More Computations

In *How to Get Fabulously Rich*, Billy wins $410,000 in the lottery. He tries to understand how much that really is. To figure out how many nickels $410,000 is, he multiplies by writing with his finger in the air. Billy figures that $410,000 is 2,050,000 nickels (page 73).

1. What numbers did Billy multiply to get his answer and why?

2. How would you determine the number of nickels in $410,000? How many are there? [Since there are 20 nickels in each dollar, $410,000 should be multiplied by 20 to figure how many nickels are in $410,000—20 × 410,000 = 8,200,000 nickels.]

3. What is the quickest way for you to do this? Air? Paper? Calculator? How can you do the computation mentally? [Multiply 410,000 by two—820,000—and add a 0 to the end—8,200,000.]

4. Can you multiply by writing in the air with your finger? Try these.

   a. 35 × 6 [210]

   b. 43 × 8 [344]

   c. 16 × 9 [144]

5. Billy also thought $410,000 would be a heap of ten-dollar bills as big as a pillow. How many ten's are in $410,000? What is the fastest way to figure the answer? [41,000; to divide by ten, move the decimal one place to the left.]

6. How many tens are in 670? 33,000? 1,000,000? 22,900? [67; 3300; 100,000; 2290]

7. The book *If You Made a Million* by David M. Schwartz (1989) helps readers understand equivalent values of money. Especially interesting is the information written on the back page, "Will a Million Dollars in Pennies Really Stack Up 95 Miles High?" Many computation activities can be formulated around the end-note information.

8. Find equivalent values for these:

   a. $625 in $5 bills [125 $5s] Can you do this division by writing in the air with your finger?

   b. $1000 in dimes [10,000 dimes] How can you do this computation mentally? [To multiply by 10, move the decimal one place to the right—add a 0.]

   c. $75 in quarters [300 quarters] Do you know any mental math shortcuts for this calculation?

   d. When making money conversions, how do you know when to multiply and when to divide? [Divide when changing to a larger denomination, as in the first problem when we converted $625 one dollars into equivalent five dollar bills. Multiply when converting to smaller denominations, as in the last two problems when we converted dollar bills to dimes and quarters.]

Computing Record-Setting Numbers

Branching off from *How to Get Fabulously Rich*, you can use *The Guinness Book of Records* (Bantam Books, yearly) to develop many creative math activities. For instance, make up computation problems like the ones below.

1. The tallest mountain in the world is Mauna Kea in Hawaii. Its total height is 33,480 feet. It rises 13,796 feet above sea level. How far below sea level is the base of the mountain?   [19,684 feet]

2. The world's highest mountain is Mount Everest at 29,029 feet above sea level.

    a. What is the difference in height from the base of the world's tallest mountain, Mauna Kea, to the peak of the world's highest mountain, Mount Everest?   [29,029 + 19,684 = 48,713 feet]

    b. To find differences we usually subtract. Why does this problem use addition?   [We are actually subtracting a negative integer. Mauna Kea is 19,684 feet *below* sea level, or −19,684. The mathematical problem is 29,029 − (−19,684) or 29,029 + 19,684. Subtracting a negative integer is the same as adding a positive one. If students have not been able to see this reasoning before, have them sketch a picture of this problem to see the meaning of it.]

    c. How many miles is this difference?   [48,713 ÷ 5280 ≈ 9.2 miles]   To what does that compare? What is about nine miles from your school?

3. The deepest part of the ocean is in the Mariana Trench in the Pacific Ocean. It is about 35,813 feet below sea level.

    a. What is the difference between the highest peak on earth and the deepest part of the ocean?   [35,813 − (−29 029) = 35,813 + 29,029 = 64,842 feet]

    b. How many miles is that?   [64 842 ÷ 5280 ≈ 12.3 miles]   To what does that compare? What is about twelve miles from your school?

    FYI If you dropped a one-kilogram (2.2 pound) ball of steel into the water at the Mariana Trench, it would take about an hour to hit the seabed.

Using Resources for Computations

Have students write computation problems for each other using *The Guinness Book of Records* or almanacs as resources. Note that some students create problems with no meaning, such as: "Multiply the number of letters in the longest name (Rhoshandiatellyneshiaunneveshenk Koyaanisquatsiuth Williams) by the numbers of letters in your name." Discuss with students the need to ask themselves, Does this have meaning? Does this make sense?

Example

The Moscow Metro train system had 3.3 billion passenger trips yearly at its peak. About how many trips were made each day on the trains? What is the best way to calculate this? Paper and pencil? Calculator? How will you know that your answer is reasonable? How will you know that it is correct?

Memorization in Mathematics

Look up the word "memorization" in *The Guinness Book of Records* index to see what kinds of things people have committed to memory. Ask students:

1. Why is memorization helpful in mathematics?

2. What things should be memorized?

3. What would be most helpful for you to memorize?

4. How will we work on that?

5. By when do you think you can have that memorized?

Minimally, students should have memorized all the fact families. Students know that addition and subtraction are related, as are multiplication and division. By memorizing one fact, they can know the other three related facts.

Examples

Addition/Subtraction   *Multiplication/Division*

$$6 + 7 = 13$$ $$6 \times 7 = 42$$
$$7 + 6 = 13$$ $$7 \times 6 = 42$$
$$13 - 6 = 7$$ $$42 \div 6 = 7$$
$$13 - 7 = 6$$ $$42 \div 7 = 6$$

Memorization Helps Make Math Easy

Memorization is not always necessary, but it expedites math computation. For example, after students have experienced enough activities to know and understand the relationship between fractions, decimals, and percents, memorizing equivalents will save them time and computation for the rest of their lives. Use activities such as the following:

1. Webbing is usually used in language arts to help students understand relationships in concepts. Webs also can be used to help students visualize and understand

relationships in numbers. Have students work as a whole class or in groups to create fraction/decimal/percent webs on large sheets of paper which can be displayed on the walls. If the work is done in small groups, discuss, modify, and add to the webs as a whole class.

Sample of Student Work

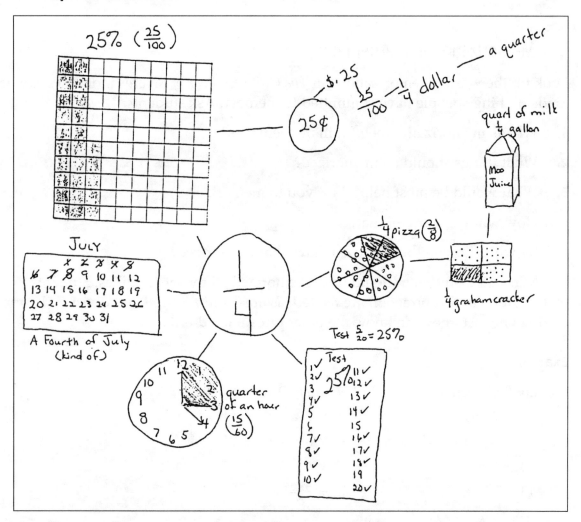

2. Make copies of Figure 2.1, Percentages of Tangram Shapes, for the students and have them determine the percentage of the square that each tangram piece covers. Some students may need to cut one of the squares apart to manipulate the pieces—by covering and comparing shapes, for example—to determine their relationships to the whole. Then they convert the percentages to decimal and fraction equivalents. Answers are on page 54.

Figure 2.1 Reproducible
Percentages of Tangram Shapes

Directions Determine what percentage of the square each shape occupies. If you need to, cut one square apart to compare the shapes to each other. Then label each shape with its percentage. Write an explanation of how you figured each shape's percentage. Then list each percentage with its fraction and decimal equivalent.

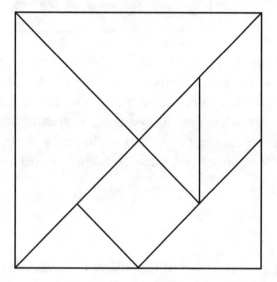

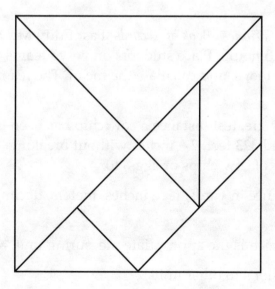

Answers for Figure 2.1

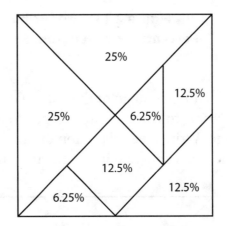

$25\% = .25 = \frac{1}{2}$
$12.5\% = .125 = \frac{1}{8}$
$6.25\% = .0625 = \frac{1}{16}$

3. Make a copy of Figure 2.2 for students to help them memorize equivalents. Modify the chart for your own use. Memorizing only the fourths (¼, ½, ¾) may be enough to begin. Some teachers start with the fourths and the tenths. Students should memorize only what they understand. Knowing that $\frac{7}{8} = 87.5\%$ without understanding it is a meaningless endeavor. To check for understanding, have students explain why some fractions, such as $\frac{6}{8}$ and $\frac{2}{10}$, are missing from the chart.

Mathematical Competitions

Students can create their own competitions using *Guinness* records as models to incorporate the concepts you are teaching at the present time.

Examples

1. **Averaging** In *The Guinness Book of Records*, Fast Eddy McDonald looped his yo-yo 21,663 times in 3 hours. Place students on yo-yo teams, count the total number of each teams' loops, and calculate the mean. The team with the highest average wins.

2. **Measurement** The greatest distance a cow chip has been thrown is 266 feet. An egg has been tossed 323 feet, 2½ inches without breaking. Have students toss Frisbees® (in place of cow chips or eggs) to:

   • Measure distance in yards, feet, inches, meters, decimeters, centimeters, and millimeters.

   • Determine which is the appropriate measuring unit.

   • Make conversions to other units.

   • Find the difference between tosses.

   • Make charts or graphs using the toss data.

   • Find mean, median, and mode.

Figure 2.2 Reproducible
Fraction, Decimal, and Percent Equivalents

Name	Fraction	Decimal	Percent
one-half	½	.50	50%
one-fourth	¼	.25	25%
three-fourths	¾	.75	75%
one-third	⅓	.33⅓ or $.\overline{3}$	33⅓% or $33.\overline{3}$%
two-thirds	⅔	.66⅔ or $.\overline{6}$	66⅔% or $66.\overline{6}$%
one-fifth	⅕	.20	20%
two-fifths	⅖	.40	40%
three-fifths	⅗	.60	60%
four-fifths	⅘	.80	80%
one-eighth	⅛	.12½ or .125	12½% or 12.5%
three-eighths	⅜	.37½ or .375	37½% or 37.5%
five-eighths	⅝	.62½ or .625	62½% or 62.5%
seven-eighths	⅞	.87½ or .875	87½% or 87.5%
one-tenth	1/10	.10	10%
three-tenths	3/10	.30	30%
seven-tenths	7/10	.70	70%
nine-tenths	9/10	.90	90%
one whole	1	1.00	100%

Probabilities

In *How to Get Fabulously Rich*, Billy plans to win the lottery, but the odds on his winning are twelve million to one. Billy's uncle has an excellent explanation about winning anything when the probability is $\frac{1}{12,000,000}$ (one in twelve million). Read pages 13 and 14 for this humorous and vivid comparison.

When we talk about chances of winning, we are talking about probability. How likely is it that an outcome will occur?

$$P = \frac{\text{number of favorable outcomes}}{\text{number of possible outcomes}}$$

For instance, when you flip a coin and someone yells, "Heads!" what is the probability it will come up heads?

$$P = \frac{\text{number of favorable outcomes}}{\text{number of possible outcomes}} = \frac{1}{2}$$

Probabilities can be expressed as fractions or ratios, so the probability in this example is ½ or one in two (also noted as 1 : 2). We can express probability on a number line.

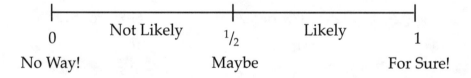

| 0 | Not Likely | ½ | Likely | 1 |

No Way!   Maybe   For Sure!

1. Where does the probability of flipping heads go on the number line?
   [in the middle]

2. How would you describe the chance that it will come up heads?
   [Sample answers: it might, it might not; 50 : 50.]

3. Where would Billy's chances of winning the lottery go on the number line?
   [very close to the zero]

4. How would you describe the probability of winning the lottery?
   [It's almost impossible.]

Probabilities in Games

Let's see how probabilities play a hand in games that kids play.

1. To start a board game, the kids place six different-colored board markers in a bag and each child pulls out one. The red always starts first.

    a. What is the probability of drawing the red marker?   [¹⁄₆ or one in six]

    b. Where would that go on the number line?   [nearer the zero]

    c. How good are the chances of getting the red?   [not very good]

2. When drawing from a 52-card deck, what is the probability of drawing:

    a. The Ace of Spades?   [¹⁄₅₂]

    b. A king?   [⁴⁄₅₂]

    c. A face card?   [¹⁶⁄₅₂]

    d. A numbered card?   [³⁶⁄₅₂]

3. Where on the number line is the chance of drawing:

    a. The Ace of Spades?   [close to zero]

    b. A numbered card?   [between ¹⁄₂ and 1]

4. Write a statement comparing the probability of drawing the Ace of Spades to the probability of drawing a numbered card.   [Sample answer: The chances of drawing the Ace of Spades are very unlikely, but the chances of drawing a numbered card are more likely.]

Probability Experiment

Give each group of students a deck of cards and have them record the results of fifty-two independent draws. After each card is drawn, it must be returned to the deck and the deck reshuffled before another draw is made.

1. Out of fifty-two draws, how many times were the following cards drawn?

    a. The Ace of Spades

    b. A king

    c. A face card

    d. A numbered card

2. How do the results compare with the mathematical predictions of probabilities in problem 2 of Probabilities in Games?

3. Compile all groups' tallies into a whole-class tally.

4. Each group had fifty-two draws. How many draws are represented by the whole class?   [Sample answer: Five groups would be 260 (5 × 52) draws.]

5. Express each total outcome as a fraction with 260 (or whatever your class total is) as the denominator and the number of times each was actually drawn as the numerator.

6. How can you compare how close the actual outcomes are to the predicted outcomes? Possible ways to compare:

    *   Convert ½₂, ⁴/₅₂, ¹⁶/₅₂, and ³⁶/₅₂ to the equivalent fractions ⁵/₂₆₀, ²⁰/₂₆₀, ⁸⁰/₂₆₀, and ¹⁸⁰/₂₆₀ (or whatever your equivalents are) and compare the actual number of draws to these numerators.

    *   Or use a calculator to convert ½₂, ⁴/₅₂, ¹⁶/₅₂, and ³⁶/₅₂ to the decimal fractions .02, .08, .31, and .69. Then convert outcome fractions to decimal fractions to see if they compare closely.

Related Books

Birdseye, Tom. *I'm Going to Be Famous*. New York: Holiday House, 1986.

Cushman, Jean. *Do You Wanna Bet? Your Chance to Find Out About Probability*. New York: Clarion Books, 1991.

Ericksen, Donna Bird, Martha L. Frank, and Ryan Kelly. "WITPO (What Is the Probability Of." *The Mathematics Teacher*, April 1991, pp. 258–265.

The Guinness Book of Records. New York: Bantam Books, yearly.

Schwartz, David M. *If You Made a Million*. New York: Lothrop, Lee, & Shepard Books, 1989.

Stenmark, Jean Kerr, Virginia Thompson, and Ruth Casey. "Rolling Records—Steps I, II, and III." *Family Math*. Berkeley, California: Lawrence Hall of Science, 1986.

The Westing Game

by Ellen Raskin
New York: E. P. Dutton, 1978

After eccentric millionaire Samuel W. Westing dies, an unlikely group of heirs is brought together to solve the mystery of his death before they can claim their inheritance. The heirs are assigned partners and each pair is given $10,000 to solve the mystery. Turtle Wexler, the youngest heir, outwits the others in this serious game.

The Westing Game is an excellent mystery for middle schoolers and can be read as a group novel. For assistance in teaching, use *The Westing Game: A Study Guide* by Beatrice G. Davis (1984). Except for the sections on playing the stock market, there is little actual math in *The Westing Game*, but you can find it everywhere, just as you can in real life. Use the activities written here as models for making math links with literature and with real life. When you find references to math topics, stop and make it a teachable moment.

Topic Business math

Objective To use real-world math in everyday situations

Applicable NCTM Standards 1, 2, 4, 5, 6, 7, 9

Calculating Tips

The residents of Sunset Towers eat many of their meals on the fifth floor at Shin Hoo's Restaurant. Practice calculating food bill totals, including the tax and tip. Make copies of the Chinese restaurant menu for the students, Figure 2.3, or find paper take-out menus from a restaurant in your neighborhood or city. Put students in groups and have them decide what to order, total the bill, add sales tax, and calculate the tip. Now have them decide how to split the bill. Will each person pay his own share or will they split it evenly? All work must be recorded and handed in.

FAMILY DINNERS

$16.25 for Two Persons

Red Lantern Dinner
Soup: Won Ton Soup
Appetizer: Egg Roll and Barbecue Pork, Fried Shrimp
Entrees: Steak Kow (Chunk of Steak with Mixed Vegetables)
Sweet & Sour Pork or Chicken
Pork Fried Rice

HOUSE DINNER

$8.95 Per Person
(Minimum Service for Two)

Soup: Won Ton Soup
Appetizer: Pu Pu Platter
Entrees: Each person choose one entree below

Moo Gao Gai Pan
Sweet Sour Pork or Chicken
★ Red Lantern Beef
Cashew Nut Shrimp
★ Kung Pao Chicken
★ Sesame Beef or Chicken
Vegetables Beef
Happy Family
Shrimp with Lobster Sauce

SOUPS

1. Egg Drop Soup (For One Person) 1.25
2. Won Ton Soup (For One Person) 1.50
3. Hot and Sour (For One Person) 1.50
4. San Shan Soup (For Two Persons) 4.25
5. Vegetables and Bean Curd Soup 3.25

HOT APPETIZERS

Pu Pu Platter
(Minimum for Two) 7.50
1. **Combination Tray** (For Two Persons) 7.95
   Egg Roll (2), Fried Shrimp (4), Barbecue Ribs (2), Fried Won Ton (4), Barbecue Pork (2), Beef Teriyaki (2).
2. **Egg Roll** (2) 1.80
3. **Fried Won Ton** (10) 1.80
4. **Pot Stickers** (6) 3.95

★ Hot and Spicy

HOT APPETIZERS

5. **Barbecued Spare Ribs** (4) (Fresh Grilled) 4.50
6. **Beef Teriyaki** (6) (Fresh Grilled) 3.95
7. **Fried Chicken Wings** (6) 3.50
8. **Barbecued Pork** (Fresh Grilled) 3.50
9. **Fried Shrimp** (7) 4.50
10. **Fried Crab Cheese Won Ton** 3.95

PORK

1. **Mo-Shu Pork** (4 Crepes) 6.50
   Shredded Pork cooked with Eggs, Cabbage, and Bamboo Shoots in a Special Sauce, skillfully rolled in wafer thin Chinese Crepes.
2. **Sweet & Sour Pork** 5.80
   Deep Fried Pork blended with our own Sweet and Sour Sauce.
3. **Pork and Snow Peas** 6.20
   Sliced Pork sautéed with Snow Peas, Bamboo and Watercress in Chinese Sauce.
★4. **Twice Cooked Pork** 6.00
   Sliced Pork cooked and then sautéed with Chinese Cabbage with a mix of Bamboo Shoots and Green Pepper in a Hot Spicy Sauce.
★5. **Kung Pao Pork** 6.00
   Diced Pork sautéed with Red Chili Pepper and Spicy Sauce.
6. **Pork with Black Mushrooms** 6.00
   Sliced Pork sautéed with Chinese Mushrooms, Snow Peas, and Bamboo Shoots in a Brown Sauce.

BEEF

7. **Broccoli with Beef** 6.00
★8. **Kung Pao Beef** 6.00
   Tenderloin Beef, Bamboo Shoots, Celery and Peanuts sautéed with Hot Spicy Szechuan Sauce.
9. **Green Pepper Tomato Beef** 6.50
★10. **Curry Beef** 6.00
★11. **Szechuan Beef** 6.00
   Sliced Beef sautéed with Cabbage in a Hot Spicy Sauce.
12. **Vegetables Beef** 6.00
★13. **Mongolian Beef** 6.75
   Sliced beef marinated in Mongolian Sauce, sautéed with Scallions. Recommended.
★14. **Red Lantern Beef** 7.75
15. **Steak Kow** 7.00
   Chunk of Steak with Assorted Vegetables.
16. **Cashew Nut Beef** 6.00
★17. **Hunan Beef** 7.00
★ **Sesame Beef** 7.00

★ Hot and Spicy

POULTRY

18. **Sweet and Sour Chicken** 5.80
19. **Red Lantern Chicken** 6.50
20. **Cashew Nut Chicken** 6.00
21. **Lemon Chicken** 7.00
★22. **Kung Pao Chicken** 6.00
   Diced Chicken sautéed with Dried Chili Peppers, Roasted Peanuts, and Spicy Hot Sauce.
23. **Almond Chicken** 6.00
★24. **Curry Chicken** 6.50
★25. **Yue-Shen Chicken** 6.00
   Fresh Chicken sautéed with Water Chestnuts and Celery in Hot Spicy Szechuan Sauce.
26. **Moo Goo Gai Pan** 6.00
   Tender and sliced White Meat with Snow Peas, Mushrooms, Broccoli, and Bamboo Shoots in a Chinese white sauce.
★27. **Ta Chien Chicken** 6.00
28. **Chicken With Garlic Sauce** 6.00
   Sliced Chicken sautéed with Onions and Black Bean Sauce.
29. **Broccoli Chicken** 6.00
30. **Chicken With Snow Peas** 6.20
31. **Double Happiness** 6.25
   Chicken and Fine Cut Pork with Assorted Vegetables.
32. **Crispy Duck** (Half) 8.25
   Duck marinated in Chef's Special Sauce, steamed and then deep fried to crispness.
33. **Sweet & Sour Duck** (Half) 8.25
34. **Peking Duck** (Whole Duck) 19.95
★ **Sesame Chicken** 6.75

SEAFOOD

35. **Sweet & Sour Shrimp** 6.00
★36. **Kung Pao Shrimp** 7.00
37. **Shrimp and Chicken Combination** 7.00
   A combination of Shrimp and Chicken sautéed with a Brown Sauce.
38. **Cashew Nut Shrimp** 7.00
39. **Mo-Shu Shrimp** (4 Crepes) 7.20
   Shrimp, Eggs, Bamboo Shoots, and Onions blended in a special sauce and skillfully rolled in Chinese Crepes.
★40. **Prawns A La Peking** 7.50
41. **Snow Peas With Shrimp** 7.20
   Fresh Shrimp sautéed with Snow Peas and Spices. Simmered in a delicate White Sauce.
★42. **Szechuan Shrimp** 7.00
43. **Shrimp With Lobster Sauce** 7.20
   Fresh Shrimp sautéed with Bamboo Shoots, Mushrooms, and Green Peas in a delightful White Sauce.
★ **Shrimp and Chicken Teriyaki** 7.25

★ Hot and Spicy

Figure 2.3 Reproducible
Chinese Restaurant Menu

Directions

1. **Each person makes his meal selections.**

2. Total the food costs.

3. Calculate the sales tax and add it to the food cost. For example, 7% tax means you must find 7% of the total (7% × total).

   - To figure by pencil and paper, multiply the food cost by the decimal equivalent of 7% or .07.

   - To figure by calculator, enter the food cost, $25.00 for instance, and multiply by 7%.   (25 ⊠ 7 ⊠%)   The display is the tax amount.
     If your calculator does not have a ⊠% key, use the same procedure on the calculator as you would with pencil and paper: 25 ⊠ .07 ⊟ _____ .

   - To estimate sales tax that is close to 5%, mentally compute 10% and halve that amount to get 5%. For example, if the bill is $14.00, find 10% by moving the decimal point one place to the left. Ten percent of $14.00 is $1.40. Five percent is half that amount or $.70.

Mental Math Calculations

In the United States, the standard tip is 15% of the bill before the tax is added. Tips are easy to calculate using mental math. Remember that 15% is the same as 10% plus 5%. To figure 10% of a $25.00 bill ($25.00 × .10), move the decimal one place to the left: $2.50. Now figure the remaining 5% (half of 10%) by finding half of the 10% amount: Half of $2.50 is $1.25. Add the 10% amount and the 5% amount to compute the 15% tip: $2.50 + $1.25 = $3.75.

1. Mentally calculate 15% tips for these food bills:

   a. $30.00   [$3.00 + $1.50 = $4.50]

   b. $15.00   [$1.50 + $.75 = $2.25]

   c. $100.00   [$10.00 + $5.00 = $15.00]

2. How would you find 15% on a calculator?   [food cost ⊠ 15 ⊠% or food cost ⊠ .15]

3. What is the entire meal's cost and how will you split it? Estimate each person's share? Divide it evenly? Compute with pencil and paper? Compute with a calculator?

Judge Ford, one of the heirs in *The Westing Game,* is a generous tipper. She probably leaves a 20% tip. At very nice dinner restaurants and for exceptional service, many people leave a 20% tip. Twenty percent is easy to determine. Because 20% is two times 10%, just figure 10% and double it. Twenty percent of $20.00 = $2.00 + $2.00 = $4.00. (For figures more difficult to work with, such as $17.63, round to the nearest dollar—$18.00. Twenty percent of $18.00 = $1.80 + $1.80 = $3.60.)

4.   Figure 20% tips for these food bills:

    a. $18.77   [$18.77 ≈ $19.00; $1.90 + $1.90 = $3.80]

    b. $53.22   [$53.22 ≈ $53.00; $5.30 + $5.30 = $10.60]

    c. $6.90   [$6.90 ≈ $7.00; $0.70 + $0.70 = $1.40]

The Stock Market

The Westing Game's protagonist, Turtle Wexler, thinks that the clues she has been given to solve the mystery indicate that she is to use the $10,000 to play the stock market. To learn more about how the stock market works, read books such as the ones listed in Related Books at the end of this section.

1.   Turtle buys $3000 worth of stocks and pays a broker a $90 commission. What percentage of the investment does the broker charge for his commission?

    Clue Set up a proportion problem:

$$\frac{90}{3000} = \frac{n}{100}$$

    Ask, 90 is to 3000 as what is to 100? Cross products are equal, so:

$$90 \times 100 = 3000n$$
$$9000 = 3000n$$
$$n = 3$$
$$\frac{n}{100} = \frac{3}{100} = 3\%$$

    To figure percentages easily, you can do the cross-product computations on a calculator: (90 × 100) ÷ 3000 = 3.

2.   Compute the percentage of commission on these transactions:

    a.   A broker charges you $200 when you buy $5000 worth of stocks. What is his commission?   [4%—$200 is to 5000 as *n* is to 100]

b. Sam pays a broker $77.50 when he buys $1550 worth of stocks. What is the broker's commission?   [5%—77.50 is to 1550 as *n* is to 100]

c. Ms. Washington writes her broker a check for $206 when she spends $200 in stock market purchases.   [3%—6 is to 200 as *n* is to 100]

3. Turtle buys stock in SEA because one of her clues is "sea." She buys 200 shares at $15.25 a share. How much does she spend?   [$15.25 × 200 = $3050]

4. Look at the reading from the screen in the broker's office on page 81 of *The West-ing Game*. SEA stock is at $8½. That means that right now SEA sells for $8.50 a share. If Turtle were to sell her stock now, how much money would she get? [$8.50 × 200 = $1700.]

5. Show how Turtle explains her loss.   [$3050 − $1700 = $1350]

6. Turtle says the reading "SEA 5$8½" means that 500 shares of SEA was traded at $8.50 a share. Explain what the other readings mean:

a. MGC 2$14   [MGC traded 200 shares at $14.00 a share.]

b. T 1000$65¼   [T traded 100,000 shares at $65.25 a share.]

c. AMI 3$19¼   [AMI traded 300 shares at $19.25 a share.]

d. I 8$22½   [I traded 800 shares at $22.50 a share.]

Understanding Stock Pages

The stock pages in a newspaper list stock information for hundreds of companies. The full name of the business usually is not printed but an abbreviation is assigned to each company. A New York Stock Exchange Report line might look like this:

52 week											
Hi	*Lo*	*Stock*	*Div*	*Yld*	*P.E.*	*100s*	*Hi*	*Lo*	*Last*	*Chg*
30¾	13⅝	AlskAir	—	—	14	531	27⅞	28½	27⅜	−½

- The first two columns, "52 week Hi" and "Lo", are the highest and lowest prices anyone paid for stock in this company in the last fifty-two weeks (year). Prices are listed in dollars and fractions of a dollar. The highest price of a share of Alaska Air stock in a year was 30¾ or $30.75. The lowest price a share in the last year was 13⅝ or $13.625. The conversions from fractions to decimal (dollars and cents) are easy to make if you have memorized equivalents. (See the web on page 52 and Figure 2.2 on page 55.) Remember these equivalents:

- ⅛ $0.125   12.5¢

- ¼ $0.25   25¢

- ⅜ $0.375   37.5¢

- ½ $0.50   50¢

- ⅝ $0.625   62.5¢

- ¾ $0.75   75¢

- ⅞ $0.875   87.5¢

- 1 $1.00   100¢

- The third column, AlskAir, is the abbreviation for Alaska Air.

- Not all companies pay dividends (Div) and not all list Yield percentages (Yld) or the Price/Earnings Ration (P.E.). These are complicated concepts. You can tell students that it is not necessary to know these now or you can find in-depth explanations in the stock market books listed at the end of the section.

- The sales column represented by "100's" is the number of shares that were traded—either bought or sold—in hundreds. The listed sales number must always be multiplied by 100; thus, 53,100 shares of Alaska Air were traded on this day.

- The second set of "Hi" and "Lo" columns show the highest price of a share of Alaska Air stock for the day was $27.875 (27⅞) and its lowest price was $28.50 (28½).

- The column titled "Last" shows the price of a share of stock at the end of the day. When the market closed, the last price—or closing price—was $27.375 (27⅜).

- The "Chg" column lists how much the price changed since the day before. The price of this stock went down $.50 (−½) from the day before.

1. If the stock closed at 27⅜, what was the previous day's closing price?
   [$1/2$ more—27$7/8$ or $27.875]

2. Make a copy of Figure 2.4, Reading the Stock Pages, for each student to practice.

Answers for Figure 2.4

1. $29.25; 2. 214,500 shares; 3. Diamond Shamrock: $34^7/8 - 23^3/8 = 11^1/2 = \$11.50$, Tupperware: $46^3/8 - 38^3/4 = 7^5/8 = \$7.625$, WalMart: $27^5/8 - 19^1/4 = 8^3/8 = \$8.375$; 4. $0.50 ($25^1/8 - 24^5/8 = ^1/2 = \$0.50$); 5. $24.875, $24.875 (Since there was no change from the previous day, opening and closing prices are the same); 6. $29.25, up $0.25, $29.00; 7. 1,599,800 shares (1,640,700 − 40,900 = 1,599,800 shares); 8. $18.75 ($46^3/8 - 27^5/8 = 18^3/4 = \$18.75$); 9. $2937.50, $2887.50, $50.00; 10. Answers will vary.

3. Look at the stock report on page 107 of *The Westing Game*. In the morning, Flora Baumbach paid $35.00 a share for WPP (Westing Paper Products). She watches it rise to 39½, then to 40, then to 40¼. If she bought 50 shares, how much money would she make in one day?

Answer

$262.50, because

$$50 \times \$35.00 = \$1750.00$$
$$50 \times \$40.25 (40^1/4) = \$2012.50$$
$$\$2012.50 - \$1750.00 = \$262.50$$

4. Keeping in mind, "Buy low; sell high," what might be going through Flora's head while she mutters, "Oh my, oh my, oh my"? Why might she be confused about what do? [Should she sell now while the price has gone up? Should she wait for the price to go higher? What if she waits and the price drops?] What would you do? Why?

5. On page 145 of *The Westing Game*, Turtle reports that their $10,000 investment increased to $11,587.50. How much money did she and Flora make? [$1587.50]

6. Turtle says it is "an appreciation of twenty-seven point eight percent." Explain what that means. [Appreciation means it went up, or gained. They made 27.8% more than they invested.]

Extension Stock Market Activity

Pair up students. Maybe you would like to use this opportunity to place dissimilar people together as Mr. Westing did when he formed teams of two to work together to solve the mystery. Pretend each pair has $10,000 dollars to invest in the stock market. They may buy as many shares of stock in as many different companies as they can afford. Also, they may buy or sell at any time they choose.

According to your students' interest levels, transactions and record keeping may be done on a daily or a weekly basis. Continue the project as long as interest remains high. Read the novel, *Hello, This Is My Father Speaking* by Mitchell Sharmat (1994) to see examples of how large amounts of money can be made (and lost) in a matter of days.

Figure 2.4 Reproducible
Reading Stock Market

52 week										
Hi	*Lo*	*Stock*	*Div*	*Yld*	*P.E.*	*100s*	*Hi*	*Lo*	*Last*	*Chg*
$34\frac{7}{8}$	$23\frac{3}{8}$	DiaShm	.56	1.9	1.9	409	$29\frac{3}{8}$	$28\frac{7}{8}$	$29\frac{1}{4}$	$+\frac{1}{4}$
$46\frac{3}{8}$	$38\frac{3}{4}$	Tuppwre	n	—	—	2145	$43\frac{5}{8}$	$42\frac{1}{2}$	$43\frac{1}{8}$	$-\frac{7}{8}$
$27\frac{5}{8}$	$19\frac{1}{4}$	WalMart	.21	.8	21	16407	$25\frac{1}{8}$	$24\frac{5}{8}$	$24\frac{7}{8}$	—

Directions Whenever possible, write your answers in dollars and cents.

1. How much was a share of Diamond Shamrock worth when the stock market closed?

2. How many shares of Tupperware were traded in this day?

3. For all three companies, compute how much their prices per share of stock have varied during the year.

4. How much did the price of WalMart stock fluctuate during this one day?

5. How much was WalMart stock worth when the stock market closed? How much was it worth at closing the day before?

6. At what price did Diamond Shamrock close? How much had it changed since the day before? What did it close at the previous day?

7. How many more shares of WalMart were sold during the day than Diamond Shamrock?

8. What is the difference between Tupperware's highest price in the past year and WalMart's highest price in the past year?

9. If you bought 100 shares of Diamond Shamrock at its highest price for the day, how much did you spend? How about if you bought 100 shares at its lowest prices for the day? How much would you save if you bought it at the lowest versus the highest point of the day?

10. A saying in the stock market is, "Buy low; sell high." What does this mean? Why is it good advice?

You may wish to take a field trip to a financial institution or a brokerage house. (Warning: Boring financial information pouring out of a poor communicator's mouth into the ears of students has been proven to be fatal.)

At the end of the project, students must sell all their stocks and present a financial report—oral, written, or both.

Olympic Math

At the end of *The Westing Game*, we learn that one of the heirs, Doug Hoo, has won an Olympic gold medal and set a record for the 1500-meter run. When you get to this part of *The Westing Game,* you may want to introduce real-life computation by using examples from the Olympics.

Find the book *Olympic Math: Gold Medal Activities and Projects for Grades 4–8* by Sharon Vogt (1996.) The Olympic Math activities involve "problem solving, reasoning, and computational skills based on Olympic scores, speeds, distances, ceremonies, Olympic life, and more." This book is real-world math. Portions of the book may be reproduced for classroom use.

Related Books

Barbarel, Linda. *Piggy Bank to Credit Card: Teach Your Child the Financial Facts of Life.* New York: Crow Trade Paperbacks, 1994.

Berg, Adriane G. and Arthur Berg Bochner. *The Totally Awesome Money Book for Kids (And Their Parents).* New York: Newmarket Press, 1993.

Bungum, Jane E. *Money and Financial Institutions.* Minneapolis, Minnesota: Lerner Publications Company, 1991.

Davis, Beatrice G. *The Westing Game: A Study Guide.* New Hyde Park, New York: Learning Links, 1984.

Dunnan, Nancy. *Banking.* Englewood Cliffs, New Jersey: Silver Burdett Press, 1990.

Little, Jeffrey B. *Bonds, Preferred Stocks, and the Money Market.* New York: Chelsea House Publishers, 1988.

Little, Jeffrey, B. *Investing and Trading.* New York: Chelsea House Publishers, 1988.

Little, Jeffrey B. *Wall Street: How It Works.* New York: Chelsea House Publishers, 1988.

Otfinoski, Steve. *The Kid's Guide to Money: Earning It, Saving It, Spending It, Growing It, Sharing It.* New York: Scholastic, 1996.

Sharmat, Mitchell. *Hello, This Is My Father Speaking.* New York: HarperCollins, 1994.

Vogt, Sharon. *Olympic Math: Gold Medal Activities and Projects for Grades 4–8.* Glenview, Illinois: GoodYear Books, 1996.

Young, Robin R. *The Stock Market.* Minneapolis, Minnesota: Lerner Publications Company, 1991.

3

Algebra, Patterns, and Functions

A Gebra Named Al

by Wendy Isdell

Minneapolis, Minnesota: Free Spirit Publishing, 1993

When Julie becomes exasperated while doing her algebra homework, she closes her eyes to rest. In a dream state, Julie enters the land of Mathematics. There she must learn about chemistry as well as mathematics in order to get back to her home.

Unless students are studying chemistry or are familiar with the Periodic Table of Elements they may lose interest in parts of this book. The teacher can read aloud passages (page numbers are noted), or the book may be assigned to students who need a challenge. Ideas presented in this lesson may be done even without the novel.

If students have read *The Phantom Tollbooth* (see Chapter 1 of this book), they can write a composition comparing and contrasting Julie's visit to the land of Mathematics in *A Gebra Named Al* to Milo's visit to the kingdom of Mathematics in *The Phantom Tollbooth*.

Topics Algebra, writing process, and vocabulary building

Objective To practice and give meaning to algebra topics

Applicable NCTM Standards 2, 3, 4, 6, 7, 8, 9, 12

The Writing Process

Julie has been holding her head up with her hand for 45 minutes trying to think of a topic to write a fantasy story about (page 1).

1. List at least five methods Julie could use to get started writing. For instance:

    • List interesting fantasy topics.

    • Free write. Write down any thoughts that come into your head even if they are rambling and don't seem to make sense.

    • Begin a web or several different webs (e.g., space travel, mythical or fantastic creatures, special powers, unexplained phenomena).

    • Cluster ideas.

    • Look at pictures in magazines or books to see if a visual image sparks an idea.

2. Choose one of these methods to find an idea to write your own fantasy story.

Take a Break from Writing and Do Some Algebra

1. Julie gives up on story writing and takes out her math homework only to find more frustration. Now, as in algebra class, she struggles with this problem: $-5 + 3(6)$. What is the solution if you work the problem (incorrectly) from left to right as Julie did?   [−12]

2. What is the solution if you work the problem (correctly) following the order of operations?   [+13]   (See pages 3 and 49 in *A Gebra Named Al* for the explanation of order of operations. See also pages 41 in this book for practice.) When following the correct order, the operations within the parentheses must be done first.

One equation that appears on pages throughout this *A Gebra Named Al* is:

$$\{3[3 + (2 \times 6)]\} + [4(13 - 6)]$$

This expression uses symbols other than parentheses—( ). These symbols—[ ]—are called brackets. These symbols—{ }—are called braces. They perform the same functions that parentheses do, and the calculations within them are performed from the inside out in this order: parentheses first, brackets second, braces third. Like this: { [( )] }. Keep in mind what Julie says on page 49: "You start at the innermost, do all the work there, and work outward."

Example $\{3[3 + (2 \times 6)]\} + [4(13 - 6)]$

$\{3[3 + (2 \times 6)]\} = \{3[3 + (12)]\}$	Solve the addend on the left by starting inside the parentheses.
$\{3[3 + (12)]\} = \{3[15]\}$	Then solve within the brackets.
$\{3[15]\} = 45$	Last, solve within the braces.

The expression is now: $45 + [4(13 - 6)]$.

$[4(13 - 6)] = [4(7)]$	Solve for the addend on the right by starting inside the parentheses.
$[4(7)] = 28$	Then solve within the brackets.

The expression is now: $45 + 28$.

$45 + 28 = 73$	Now the expression can be evaluated by adding the solved addends. *Evaluating* means finding the value of an algebraic expression.

Summary $\{3[3 + (2 \times 6)]\} + [4(13 - 6)] = 45 + 28 = 73$

3. Evaluate the following expressions remembering the order of operations and to "start at the innermost, do all the work there, and work outward."

   a. $6 + -4(5 - 2)$ [−6]

   b. $-3(-1 - 4) - 17$ [−2]

   c. $6 + [2(8 + 1) - 4]$ [20]

   d. $\{8[2 + (4 \times 7)]\} - \{7 + [(9 \times 3) - 1] - 3\}$ [210]

   e. $[6(4 + 7) - 5] + \{[40(0 + 4)] - 3\}$ [218]

Vocabulary Building

In *A Gebra Named Al*, Julie discovers a dark portal with a white cloud floating in front of it in her room (page 4).

1. What is a portal? Look up the word's origin (etymology) in a dictionary. It is located within brackets following the pronunciation. Can you find in the etymology that the word portal originates from a Latin word, *porta*, meaning door?

2. Find another word in the dictionary that begins with "port" and has a meaning associated with door.   [Be careful; many words beginning with "port" are related to carrying or transporting because their root word is *portare* which is Latin for "to carry."]

3. Al Gebra teaches Julie how to pronounce his name (page 10). His pronunciation sounds a lot like the original words for algebra from the Arabic language. Look up the etymology of algebra.

   a. What are the original words?   [al-jabr]

   b. What does this mean?   [reunion of broken parts; definitions may vary]

   c. How does the original meaning fit this particular field of mathematics? How can parts of math be broken? How can they be reunited?

Breaking Parts in Math: Prime Factorization

Any composite number can be expressed as the product of prime numbers. The composite number is "broken down" to prime numbers. One way to break them down is to use factor trees.

Examples

```
       84                        525
      /\                        /\
    2 × 42                    5 × 105
    /   /\                    /    /\
  2 × 2 × 21                5 × 5 × 21
  /   /   /\                /   /   /\
2 × 2 × 3 × 7            5 × 5 × 3 × 7

  2² × 3 × 7               3 × 5² × 7
```

1. Use factor trees to find the prime factorization of the following numbers:

   a. 63 $[3^2 \times 7]$

   b. 56 $[2^3 \times 7]$

   c. 900 $[2^2 \times 3^2 \times 5^2]$

   d. 624 $[2^4 \times 3 \times 13]$

2. Use factor trees to find the prime number for n that will make each equation true.

   a. $72 = 2^3 \times n^3$ $[n = 3]$

   b. $350 = 2 \times n^2 \times 7$ $[n = 5]$

    c. $2^3 \times n \times 7 = 168$ [n = 3]

    d. $2 \times 5^2 \times n = 550$ [n = 11]

    e. $360 = n^3 \times 3^2 \times 5$ [n = 2]

3.   Use factor trees to find the number for each exponent that will make the equation true.

    a. $3 \times 5^n = 75$ [n = 2]

    b. $2^n \times 3 \times 5 = 120$ [n = 3]

    c. $297 = 3^n \times 11$ [n = 3]

    d. $3^n = 243$ [n = 5]

    e. $2^2 \times 3^n = 324$ [n = 4]

When these broken parts (factorizations) are reunited (multiplied) they become the original composite number.

Variables in Algebra

The study of algebra works not only with broken parts, but also with unknown or missing parts, such as in the equations (number sentences) above. The missing part can be replaced with a letter called a variable. Look at the equations below:

$p + 18 = 21$ $r - 23 = 11$ $6q = 24$ $m \div 4 = 24$

The equals sign shows that the expressions on each side are equal; they represent the same number. Both sides balance as if they are on a balance scale.

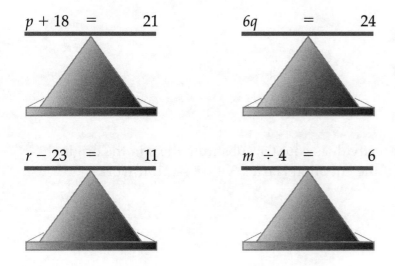

1. To figure out what number the variable represents, we try to find a way to make the letter stand alone on one side of the balance. Then we read the number or expression on the other side of the balance to see what it equals.

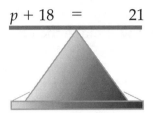

$$p + 18 \quad = \quad 21$$

- On the balance scale above, how can we make p stand alone?   [By taking off (subtracting) the 18.]

- But if we subtract 18 from one side only, the equation no longer balances. The right side is 18 too light.

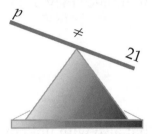

- To keep an equation balanced, whatever is done to one side must also be done to the other. So we must subtract 18 from each side.

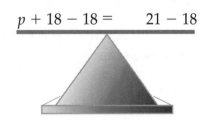

$$p + 18 - 18 = \quad 21 - 18$$

$$p + 18 - \mathbf{18} = 21 - \mathbf{18}$$
$$p + 0 = 3$$
$$p = 3$$

- To check to see if the p really does equal 3, substitute the p in the original equation with 3 to see if the equation is true: $3 + 18 = 21$. It works.

2. On page 64 of *A Gebra Named Al,* Julie and Tritium talk about addition and subtraction being perfect opposites. They say that multiplication and division also are perfect opposites. What do they mean?   [They are inverse, or opposite operations. One can "undo" the other. Subtracting a number will undo adding it, and adding a number will undo subtracting it. Dividing a number will undo multiplying by the same number, and multiplying will undo dividing by the same number.]

3. In the equation above, $p + 18 = 21$, we undid adding the eighteen by performing the inverse operation and subtracting 18 in order to get the p to stand alone.

   a. In the equation $r - 23 = 11$, how can we undo subtracting 23 to make the r stand alone?   [Add 23.]

   b. If we add 23 to one side, what must we do to the other side?   [Add 23]

   c. Show the work to solve for the variable:

$$r - 23 = 11$$
$$r - 23 + 23 = 11 + 23$$
$$r - 0 = 34$$
$$r = 34$$

   Now substitute the variable with the solution to prove the result:

   $34 - 23 = 11$ Correct.

4. Answer the following questions for the equation $6q = 24$:

   a. How can we undo multiplying by 6 to get the q to stand alone?   [Divide by 6.]

   b. If we divide one side by 6, what must we do to the other side?   [Divide by 6.]

   c. Show the work to solve for the variable:

$$6q = 24$$
$$\frac{6q}{6} = \frac{24}{6}$$
$$q = 4$$

   Now substitute the variable with the solution to prove the result:

   $6 \times 4 = 24$ Correct.

5. Answer the following questions for the equation $m \div 4 = 24$:

   a. How can we undo dividing by 4 to get the m to stand alone?   [Multiply by 4.]

   b. If we multiply one side by 4, what must we do to the other side?
   [Multiply by 4.]

c.   Show the work to solve for the variable:

$m \div 4 = 24$

$\dfrac{m}{4} \times 4 = 24 \times 4$

$m = 96$

Now substitute the variable with the solution to prove $96 \div 4 = 24$.

6.   Solve for the following variables:

a. $24 + u = 41$ [$u = 17$]

b. $63 = 31 + t$ [$t = 32$]

c. $92 = v - 17$ [$v = 109$]

d. $b - 6 = 20$ [$b = 26$]

e. $13h = 39$ [$h = 3$]

f. $51 = 17c$ [$c = 3$]

g. $k \div 5 = 95$ [$k = 475$]

h. $202 = w \div 27$ [$w = 5454$]

7.   Read about Julie creating food by "cubing" (pages 19–20). How does she explain it? Does that explanation make sense to you? Why?

8.   Al says that cubing numbers is easy too. Julie already knows that a cubed number is "where you multiply a number by itself, then again" (page 19). For example:

Take a number.	Square it.	Cube it.
$3^1 = 3$	$3^2 = 9$	$3^3 = 27$

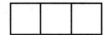 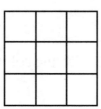 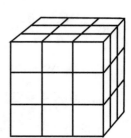

9. Have students make models of cubed numbers with math cubes or blocks or with sugar cubes. Solve the following:

   a. six cubed   [216]

   b. four cubed   [64]

   c. 2^3 [8]

   d. 10^3 [1000]

   e. 7^3 [343]

10. To figure if she has enough food left, Julie computes, "Ten cubes divided by 5 days equals two cubes a day" (page 66). Is that the same as ten cubed (10^3) divided by 5? Why?   [No. $10^3 \div 5 = 1000 \div 5 = 200$]

    Solve the following:

   a. five cubed divided by 6   [$20^5/_6$]

   b. eleven cubed divided by 3   [$443^2/_3$]

   c. $9^3 \div 3$ [243]

   d. $3^3 \div 5$ [$5^2/_5$]

   e. $4^3 \times 5^3$ [8000]

More Algebra Problems

1. As soon as she determines that there is not enough food for five days, Julie begins to think about the way cells multiply and divide (pages 67–68). In one stage of the process asters form. Julie wonders if the word "aster" is related to the word "astronaut."

   a. Is it? How could you find out?   [Look up their etymologies.]

   b. Find two other words related to their root words.   [Sample answers: asteroid and astronomy]

2. Explain what Lithium means when he says, "Subtraction is as deep as Addition is tall" (page 70).   [Answers will vary, but should contain language mentioning inverse or opposite operations.]

   Make up a similar statement about multiplication and division. Do not use the words deep and tall.

3. Al and Julie walk across the Prime Plain while they discuss both the Prime Plain and the Composite Plain. Julie concludes that the Prime Plain "can't be divided into smaller parts, but the Composite Plain can" (page 75). Explain what she means. It might be helpful to think about the factor trees in problem 1 on page 72.

4. Julie and Al talk about equations (page 83). One equation is $d = r \times t$. See *Around the World in Eighty Days,* Chapter 6, Measurement, pages 170 and 173 for "distance equals rate $\times$ time" problems.

5. In *A Gebra Named Al,* read about the tower on pages 100–101. Pay close attention to the description, and draw a picture of what this tower might look like. See the sample in the right margin.

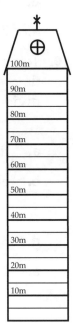

6. Read Mark and Julie's conversation on pages 102–103 about perfect squares.

    a. On graph or grid paper (see Figure 1.6, page 33), have students draw squares of numbers.

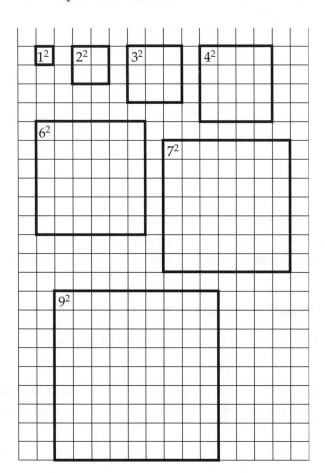

b. Then have students draw the progression of squares.

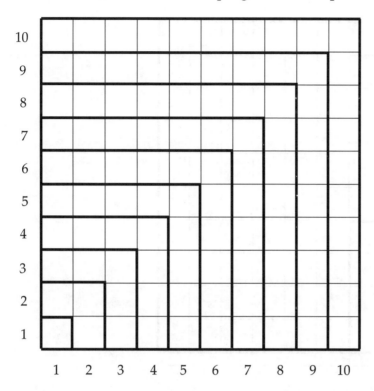

7. Lead students to discover equations such as:

$$(5 + 2)^2 = 7^2$$

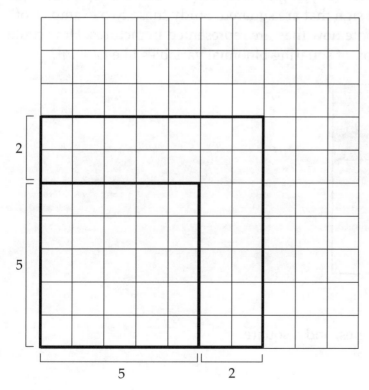

$(4 + 6)^2 = 10^2$

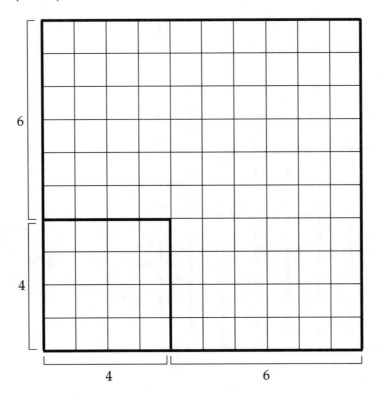

8. When Mark talks about square binomials (page 102), he is referring to equations such as the one above—two (bi-) single numbers (monomials) separated by an addition (or subtraction) sign that are squared. Study these two examples of squared binomials and note how they are represented in pictures. How could you draw a representation of squaring binomial variables like $(a + b)^2$?

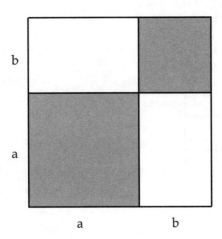

It is a square, two rectangles, and a square.

a. What is the solution to $(a + b)^2$?   [$(a + b)^2 = a^2 + 2(ab) + b^2$]

b. Draw the representation and write the same kind of solution for the numbers $(2 + 3)^2$. Look for a square, two rectangles, and a square.

Answer

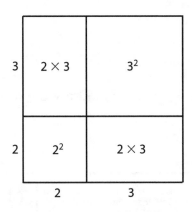

$$(2 + 3)^2 = 2^2 + 2(2 \times 3) + 3^2$$
$$= 4 + 12 + 9$$
$$= 25$$

9. **Challenge!** Mark also mentions square trinomials—three monomials. How would you draw a representation of $(a + b + c)^2$?

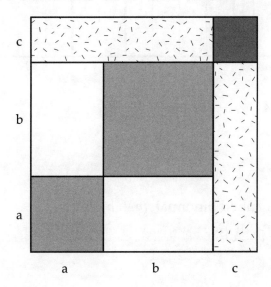

It is a square, two rectangles, another square, two more rectangles, and another square.

a. What is the solution to $(a + b + c)^2$?

Answer

$(a + b + c)^2 = a^2 + 2ab + b^2 + 2c(a + b) + c^2$
a^2 = square
$2ab$ = rectangles
b^2 = square
$2c(a + b)$ = rectangles
c^2 = square

b. Replace the variables with these numbers: $(4 + 2 + 3)^2$. Draw the representation and write a similar solution.

Answer

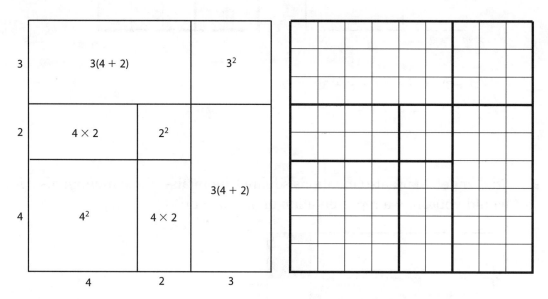

$$(4 + 2 + 3)^2 = 4^2 + 2(4 \times 2) + 2^2 + 2 \times 3(4 + 2) + 3^2$$
$$= 16 + 16 + 4 + 36 + 9$$
$$= 81$$

10. Extra Challenge!!

a. Can you draw a representation of a cubed binomial, $(a + b)^3$?

b. How about a cubed trinomial, $(a + b + c)^3$?

c. What are their solutions?

Back to Writing

1. Back home, Julie finally gets down to writing her story (*A Gebra Named Al*, page 110).

   a. What techniques does she use to try to start her writing process?
   [making a brainstormed list, free writing, drawing a cluster]

   b. How does she finally get started?   [by writing a personal experience]

2. Is there any way you could use something that really happened to you to write a fantasy story? Write it and incorporate mathematical ideas and problems into the story.

Patterns and Functions

Recognizing and understanding patterns is useful for understanding algebra. While some of the activities from *A Gebra Named Al* are more appropriate for eighth graders, younger students should be working with less symbolic activities—first by manipulating concrete objects, and then by using charts and tables such as are suggested in the following ideas. You may wish to simplify these activities, and you may choose not to progress to the symbolic level of using variables to describe functions.

Tables and Relationships

1. Have students build rectangular prisms with blocks. Have them determine how many blocks are in one layer, two layers, three layers, and so on.

2. Have students make a table to record their results of activity 1.

   Example Here is a table for a rectangular prism that measures $2 \times 3 \times 6$.

Layers	1	2	3	4	5	6
Cubes	6	12	18	24	30	36

3. How does the number of cubes relate to the number of layers?   [There are always 6 times more cubes than layers.]   If l represents the number of layers, what expression will describe the number of cubes?   [$6l$]   If c represents the number of cubes, the equation is $6l = c$.

4.   Becky and Mark agree to eat one cookie every 5 minutes. Mark doesn't know that Becky already ate three cookies before they made the agreement. How could you make a table showing the number of cookies they eat?

Mark	0	1	2	3	4	5	6
Becky	3	4	5	6	7	8	9

5.   If *m* equals the number of Mark's cookies and *b* equals the number of Becky's cookies, write an expression showing how many cookies Becky has eaten compared to Mark.   [*m* + 3]   What is the equation for the table?   [*m* + 3] = *b*

6.   Your brother says that you must give him half of your babysitting money every week or he will ruin your life.

   a.   Finish the table to determine how much you will have to pay him if you bow to his demands.

Wages	$4.00	$5.00	$6.00 ...	[... $7.00	$8.00	$9.00	$10.00]
Bribes	$2.00	$2.50	$3.00 ...	[... $3.50	$4.00	$4.50	$5.00]

   b.   Write an equation describing the sorry situation.   [*w* ÷ 2 = *b*]

7.   In each of the above situations, two quantities create a pattern. They have formed a relationship. Study the table below and find the relationship.

x	1	2	3	4	5	6	7
y	3	6	9	12	15	18	21

   a.   How is *y* related to *x*?   [Every *y* is three times *x*.]

   b.   How do you write the equation?   [3*x* = *y*]

8.   Complete the following tables and write an expression using *x* to show the value of *y*.

x	4	5	6 ...	[...7	8	9	10]
y	6	7	8 ...	[...9	10	11	12 ***x* + 2 = *y*]**

x	7	8	9	...	[... 10	11	12	13]	
y	6	7	8	...	[... 9	10	11	12	$x - 1 = y$]

x	7	14	21	...	[... 28	35	42	49]	
y	1	2	3	...	[... 4	5	6	7	$x \div 7 = y$]

Plotting Ordered Pairs on a Coordinate Plane

The intersection of a horizontal number line (called the x-axis) and a vertical number line (called the y-axis) forms a coordinate plane. The point where the axes intersect is called the origin.

All locations on the coordinate plane can be described by using the numbers along the axes. The first number, or x-coordinate, tells how far to move horizontally. The second number, or y-coordinate, tells how far to move vertically. The coordinates are written as an ordered pair (x, y).

Example

For the ordered pair $(-3, 4)$ move left on the x-axis to -3, then up vertically 4. The point $(-3, 4)$ is located as shown:

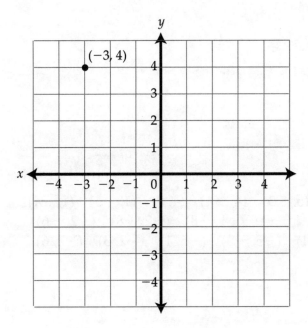

1. Hand out copies of Figure 3.1 to the students and have them identify the coordinates for the points shown. [A (−4, 0)   B (−3, 3)   C (0, 2)   D (−1, −2)   E (2, 2)   F (3, 1)   G (4, −2)   H (0, −4)]

2. Have the students identify the points of the listed coordinates in the second graph in Figure 3.1. [D (3, −2)   E (−2, 3)   B (−1, −3)   F (2, 4)   G (−3, −4)   A (2, 2)   C (−4, 1)   H (1, −2)]

3. Have students make a dot-to-dot drawing such as the one below using the grid paper, Figure 1.6, on page 33. Have them write the coordinates in the order they are drawn on a separate sheet of paper and exchange coordinates with another student. They should not show their drawings. Ask them to graph and connect the points. Both partners' drawings should be identical.

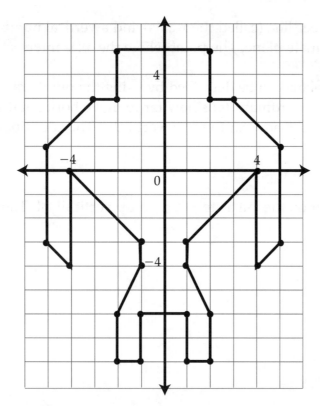

Ordered Pairs (Coordinates) for Sample
(−2, 6)   (2, 6)   (2, 3)   (3, 3)   (5, 1)   (5, −3)   (4, −4)   (4, 0)   (1, −3)   (1, −4)
(2, −6)   (2, −8)   (1, −8)   (1, −6)   (−1, −6)   (−1, −8)   (−2, −8)   (−2, −6)
(−1, −4)   (−1, −3)   (−4, 0)   (−4, −4)   (−5, −3)   (−5, 1)   (−2, 3)   (−2, 6)

Figure 3.1 Reproducible
Plotted Coordinates

1. Identify the coordinates for each point below in the following graph:

A _____   B _____   C _____   D _____   E _____

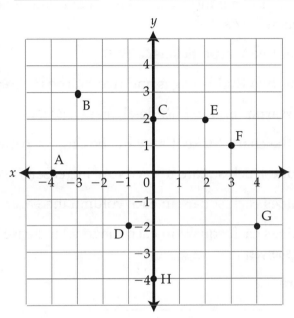

2. Name the points in the next graph which have the following coordinates:

(3, −2) _____   (−2, 3) _____   (−1, −3) _____   (2, 4) _____

(−3, −4) _____   (2, 2) _____   (−4, 1) _____   (1, −2) _____

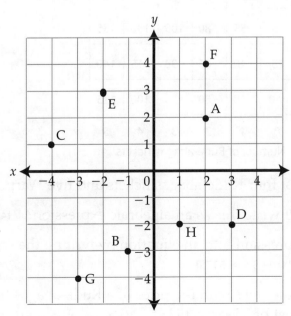

Combination Chart

Make a copy of Figure 3.2, Combination Chart, for every student. Concert tickets for the rock band Warpo sell for $15 each. Tickets for the more popular band, The Rude-abagas, sell for $25 each. By making a chart we can determine how much different combinations of tickets will cost.

1.   What is the cost of five Warpo tickets?   [$75]

2.   What is the cost of two Rude-abagas and two Warpos?   [$80]

3.   How about four Warpos and two Rude-abagas?   [$110]

4.   Fill in the rest of the chart. Make it easy by looking for patterns.

   a.   How much does each square in each row increase?   [$25]

   b.   How much does each square in each column increase?   [$15]

   c.   How much does each square in each diagonal increase? Is this true for every diagonal?   [$40; yes]

Answers for Figure 3.2

5	75	100	125	150	175	200
4	60	85	110	135	160	185
3	45	70	95	120	145	170
2	30	55	80	105	130	155
1	15	40	65	90	115	140
0	0	25	50	75	100	125
	0	**1**	**2**	**3**	**4**	**5**

Number of Warpo Tickets (vertical axis)

Number of Rude-abagas Tickets (horizontal axis)

5.   What is the cost of four Rude-abagas tickets and five Warpo tickets?   [$175]

   a.   How can you write this as an algebraic expression?   [4r + 5w]

   b.   Make the expression into an equation by writing the solution (how much they cost).   [4r + 5w = $175]

   c.   Now substitute the r with the price of a Rude-abagas ticket and substitute the w with cost of a Warpo ticket.   [(4 × $25) + (5 × $15) = $175]

   d.   Does the equation prove to be true?   [$100 + $75 = $175; yes]

Figure 3.2 Reproducible
Combination Chart

Rock Band Tickets

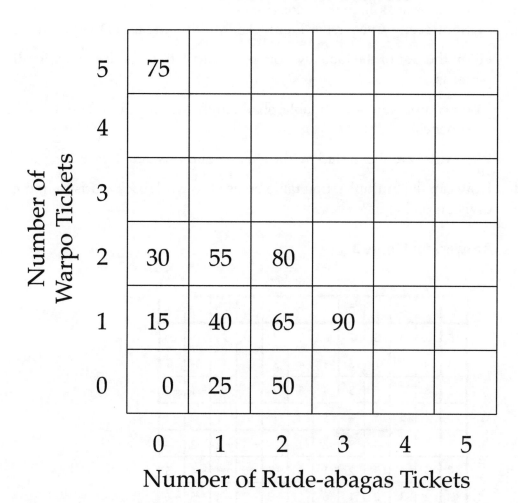

Number of Warpo Tickets

	0	1	2	3	4	5
5	75					
4						
3						
2	30	55	80			
1	15	40	65	90		
0	0	25	50			

Number of Rude-abagas Tickets

Integers Tables: Addition, Subtraction, Multiplication, and Division

Before students work on these activities they already should have been engaged in integer activities, worked on number lines, and learned integer computation rules.

1.   As you cover each skill, make a copy of either Figure 3.3, Adding Integers; Figure 3.4, Subtracting Integers; or Figure 3.5, Multiplying and Dividing Integers.

   a.   Fill in the rest of the table by doing the calculation and by following the patterns.

   b.   Upon completion of each table, shade in the negative numbers with a colored pencil.

   c.   What rules are illustrated by the shaded and unshaded parts?

   d.   How can the multiplication table be used to work backwards to figure division problems?

Answers for Figure 3.3

Second Number

+	5	4	3	2	1	0	−1	−2	−3	−4	−5
5	10	9	8	7	6	5	4	3	2	1	0
4	9	8	7	6	5	4	3	2	1	0	−1
3	8	7	6	5	4	3	2	1	0	−1	−2
2	7	6	5	4	3	2	1	0	−1	−2	−3
1	6	5	4	3	2	1	0	−1	−2	−3	−4
0	5	4	3	2	1	0	−1	−2	−3	−4	−5
−1	4	3	2	1	0	−1	−2	−3	−4	−5	−6
−2	3	2	1	0	−1	−2	−3	−4	−5	−6	−7
−3	2	1	0	−1	−2	−3	−4	−5	−6	−7	−8
−4	1	0	−1	−2	−3	−4	−5	−6	−7	−8	−9
−5	0	−1	−2	−3	−4	−5	−6	−7	−8	−9	−10

First Number

Answers for Figure 3.4

Second Number

−	5	4	3	2	1	0	−1	−2	−3	−4	−5
5	0	1	2	3	4	5	6	7	8	9	10
4	−1	0	1	2	3	4	5	6	7	8	9
3	−2	−1	0	1	2	3	4	5	6	7	8
2	−3	−2	−1	0	1	2	3	4	5	6	7
1	−4	−3	−2	−1	0	1	2	3	4	5	6
0	−5	−4	−3	−2	−1	0	1	2	3	4	5
−1	−6	−5	−4	−3	−2	−1	0	1	2	3	4
−2	−7	−6	−5	−4	−3	−2	−1	0	1	2	3
−3	−8	−7	−6	−5	−4	−3	−2	−1	0	1	2
−4	−9	−8	−7	−6	−5	−4	−3	−2	−1	0	1
−5	−10	−9	−8	−7	−6	−5	−4	−3	−2	−1	0

First Number (row label)

Answers for Figure 3.5

Second Number

×	5	4	3	2	1	0	−1	−2	−3	−4	−5
5	25	20	15	10	5	0	−5	−10	−15	−20	−25
4	20	16	12	8	4	0	−4	−8	−12	−16	−20
3	15	12	9	6	3	0	−3	−6	−9	−12	−15
2	10	8	6	4	2	0	−2	−4	−6	−8	−10
1	5	4	3	2	1	0	−1	−2	−3	−4	−5
0	0	0	0	0	0	0	0	0	0	0	0
−1	−5	−4	−3	−2	−1	0	1	2	3	4	5
−2	−10	−8	−6	−4	−2	0	2	4	6	8	10
−3	−15	−12	−9	−6	−3	0	3	6	9	12	15
−4	−20	−16	−12	−8	−4	0	4	8	12	16	20
−5	−25	−20	−15	−10	−5	0	5	10	15	20	25

First Number (row label)

**Figure 3.3 Reproducible
Adding Integers**

Second Number

+	5	4	3	2	1	0	−1	−2	−3	−4	−5
5	10	9	8	7	6	5	4	3			0
4	9					4					−1
3	8		6			3					−2
2	7					2					
1	6					1					
0	5					0					
−1	4					−1					
−2	3		1								
−3										−7	
−4					−3						
−5			−2		−4		−6				

First Number

Figure 3.4 Reproducible
Subtracting Integers

Second Number

First Number	−	5	4	3	2	1	0	−1	−2	−3	−4	−5
	5	0	1	2	3	4	5					
	4		0						6			
	3											
	2	−3										
	1											
	0											
	−1										3	
	−2				−3							
	−3									0		
	−4			−6								
	−5						−5					

Figure 3.5 Reproducible
Multiplying and Dividing Integers

Second Number

×	5	4	3	2	1	0	−1	−2	−3	−4	−5
5	25					0					
4											
3				6							
2											
1											−5
0						0					
−1											
−2	−10										
−3									9		
−4		−16						8			
−5											

First Number

Related Books

Lerner, Marcia and Doug McMullen, Jr. *Math Smart Junior: Math You'll Understand.* New York: Random House, 1995.

Sachar, Louis. *More Sideways Math from Wayside School: More Than 50 Brainteasing Math Puzzles.* New York: An Apple Paperback, Scholastic, 1994.

Figgs and Phantoms

by Ellen Raskin
New York: Puffin Books, 1989

This book written for grades 5–9 chronicles the adventures of the unusual Figg family after they leave show business and settle in the town of Pineapple.

Topic Breaking codes with letters, symbols, and numbers

Objective To compare algebra to codebreaking by solving for unknowns, using what is known to solve what is not known

Applicable NCTM Standards 1, 2, 4, 5, 8, 9

Algebra and Codebreaking

The word "algebra" is derived from the Arabian word "al-gabr," meaning "integration of broken parts." Students may be able to understand algebra more readily if they see it as a process of finding broken parts or missing pieces or as solving a mystery. It is difficult to find literature with direct references to algebra, however you can find stories and novels, such as *Figgs and Phantoms*, that entail breaking codes—finding unknowns and determining a secret message's meaning by cracking its code. (See the Related Books section for more ideas.) Students who possess these skills have an easier time deciphering algebra. Algebra and cryptology are alike—both fields are based on using what is known to solve what is not.

Practicing Unknowns in Computation

Give each student a copy of Figure 3.6 and 3.7 showing partial computation problems and have them complete them. Their practice will help you determine what they do or do not know before proceeding with the codebreaking activities.

Answers for Figure 3.6

```
    6 1 9              9 2 7            4 9 4 3
  + 3 7 2            +   6 8 8            6 3 7
    9 9 1            1 6 1 5          +   7 4 2
                                      6 3 2 2
```

```
      2 7                    6                    2 8
  ×     7            7 ) 4 2            5 ) 1 4 0
    1 8 9                4 2                1 0
                            0                  4 0
                                               4 0
                                                0
```

$39 + 48 + 5 = 16 + \boxed{76}$

$84 + \boxed{26} + 17 = 127$

$7 \times (3 + \boxed{6}) = 63$

$(2 \times \boxed{1}) + (2 \times 7) = 16$

$(9 \times \boxed{2}) + (9 \times 3) = 45$

Answers for Figure 3.7

						4	3	8	9	7	2
					×	6	1	5	2	3	6
				2	6	3	3	8	3	2	
			1	3	1	6	9	1	6	0	
		8	7	7	9	4	4	0	0		
	2	1	9	4	8	6	0	0	0		
4	3	8	9	7	2	0	0	0	0		
2	6	3	3	8	3	2	0	0	0	0	
2	7	0	0	7	1	3	7	7	3	9	2

Figure 3.6 Reproducible
Computation Practice

```
   6 1 9              □ 2 7              □ □ 4 3
 + 3 □ 2            +   6 8 □                6 3 7
   □ 9 1              1 6 □ 5          +     7 □ 2
                                            6 3 2 □
```

```
      □ □                    6                    2 8
   ×     7           7 ) □ □           5 ) □ 4 0
    1 8 9                □ □                □ □
                        ——                 ——
                          0                  □ □
                                             □ □
                                             ——
                                               0
```

$39 + 48 + 5 = 16 + \boxed{}$

$84 + \boxed{} + 17 = 127$

$7 \times (3 + \boxed{}) = 63$

$(2 \times \boxed{}) + (2 \times 7) = 16$

$(9 \times \boxed{}) + (9 \times 3) = 45$

Figure 3.7 Reproducible
Computation Practice

								8	9	7	2
					×	6	1		2	3	6
					2	6			8	3	2
				1			6	9	1		
					7	7	9	4			
			2		4	8	6	0			
					8	9	7	2			
	2			3	8	3	2				
					7	1	3	7	7		

Substitution Codes

Substitution codes are made by substituting letters, numbers, or symbols for the alphabet. For instance, at the end of Part III, Chapter 2 in *Figgs and Phantoms*, Remus "ran up and down the street screaming 6-9-18-5, 6-9-18-5. By the time Harriet Kluttz figured out that the numbers stood for letters of the alphabet, her beauty parlor had burned to the ground."

The simplest kind of substitution code is when numbers represent letters of the alphabet: A = 1, B = 2, C = 3, and so on. Students can write and decipher messages such as:

```
13-1-25 9 8-1-22-5  25-15-21-18  1-20-20-5-14-20-9-15-14
16-12-5-1-19-5  20-8-9-19  2-21-9-12-4-9-14-7  9-19
15-14 6-9-18-5 .
```
[MAY I HAVE YOUR ATTENTION PLEASE? THIS BUILDING IS ON FIRE.]

More difficult cryptograms are made by substituting each letter of the alphabet with another randomly chosen letter. Example: A = K, B = F, C = I, D = O, and so on. This type of puzzle appears in many daily newspapers like this:

```
P AKJC VCCL RBN CJCUR OKI JAPV DCCH.
```

It would take a long time to solve this cryptogram by guessing. A helpful clue is in the table of frequencies—a list of letters that tells how often each letter is used in the English language. People who are familiar with word construction, however, do not use a table.

Table of Frequencies
Letter Occurrence per 100 Words

Rank	Letter	Occurrence	Rank	Letter	Occurrence	Rank	Letter	Occurrence
1	E	13	10	D	4	19	W	Less than 2
2	T	10	11	L	3	20	B	
3	A	8	12	F	3	21	V	
4	O	8	13	C	3	22	K	
5	N	7	14	M	3	23	X	
6	R	7	15	U	2	24	J	
7	I	6	16	G	2	25	Q	
8	S	6	17	Y	2	26	Z	
9	H	5	18	P	2			

Since the letter "E" occurs most frequently in the English language, begin to solve the puzzle by substituting the most recurring letter with the letter "E":

```
P  AKJC  VCCL  RBN  CJCUR  OKI  JAPV  DCCH.

_  ___E  _EE_  ___  E_E__  ___  ____  _EE_.
```

- The first word is either "I" or "A."

- Two words have EE in the middle. Solution possibilities could be: BEEN, DEER, FEEL, HEEL, KEEL, PEEK, REEL, REEK, SEEN, TEEN, WEEK.

- If the first word is "I," a verb should follow. Possibilities include: I HAVE SEEN, I HAVE BEEN.

- Try one possibility to see if the other letter substitutions could make sense.

```
P  AKJC  VCCL  RBN  CJCUR  OKI  JAPV  DCCH.

I  HAVE  SEEN  HI_  EVE__  _A_  _HIS  _EE_.
```

Solution I HAVE SEEN HIM EVERY DAY THIS WEEK.

Edgar Allan Poe used this type substitution cipher system in his mystery story "The Gold Bug." (See Related Books section for a partial list of anthologies.) The story revolves around a cryptogram discovered by a character named Legrand:

```
53++x305))6*;4826)4+.);806*;48x8060))85;1+(;:+*8x83(88)5*x;
46(;88*96*?;8+(;485);5*x2:*+(;4956*2(5*_;4)808*;4069285);)
6x8)4++;1(+9;48081;8:8+1;48x85;4)485x528806*81(+9;48;(88;4(+?
34;48)4+;161;:188;+?;
```

In this cryptogram, random symbols and numbers replace letters. The 8 appears most frequently—33 times—and represents the letter "E." Poe provides the code, a frequency table, and the solution in the story. In many children's versions of "The Gold Bug," the original code and table are deleted.

Other Substitution Codes

The Polybius Square is also called the Greek Square. Over 2000 years ago, Polybius, a Greek man who worked for the Romans, devised a substitution cipher which uses symbols for each letter of the alphabet. He drew a 5 × 5 square matrix and placed one letter in each square. The Roman alphabet had only twenty-five letters, so when using the English alphabet, two letters—I and J—must share one spot in order to fit.

The Polybius Square

	1	2	3	4	5
1	A	B	C	D	E
2	F	G	H	IJ	K
3	L	M	N	O	P
4	Q	R	S	T	U
5	V	W	X	Y	Z

To encode, give the row number first and then the column number where each letter is located. The row and column number for T is 44, for E it is 15. The word TELESCOPE would be enciphered: 44 15 31 15 43 13 34 35 15.

The Pigpen Cipher

This cipher got its name because the lines of this code look like pigs in a pen. It was used by Confederate soldiers for secret messages during the American Civil War. Sometimes it is called the Mason's Cipher because at one time it was used for secret codes by the Society of Freemasons.

A message is encoded by substituting the shape of the pigpen compartment that holds that letter. This is its key:

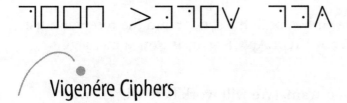

The following code is deciphered NEED MONEY NOW.

Vigenére Ciphers

In the sixteenth century, a Frenchman named Blaise de Vigenére invented and wrote about many ciphers. Three hundred years later, a mathematician at Oxford University published his own cipher based on a Vigenére table. That mathematician was Lewis Carroll, author of *Alice's Adventures in Wonderland* and *Through the Looking Glass.*

Vigenére Table

	A	B	C	D	E	F	G	H	I	J	K	L	M	N	O	P	Q	R	S	T	U	V	W	X	Y	Z	
A	a	b	c	d	e	f	g	h	i	j	k	l	m	n	o	p	q	r	s	t	u	v	w	x	y	z	A
B	b	c	d	e	f	g	h	i	j	k	l	m	n	o	p	q	r	s	t	u	v	w	x	y	z	a	B
C	c	d	e	f	g	h	i	j	k	l	m	n	o	p	q	r	s	t	u	v	w	x	y	z	a	b	C
D	d	e	f	g	h	i	j	k	l	m	n	o	p	q	r	s	t	u	v	w	x	y	z	a	b	c	D
E	e	f	g	h	i	j	k	l	m	n	o	p	q	r	s	t	u	v	w	x	y	z	a	b	c	d	E
F	f	g	h	i	j	k	l	m	n	o	p	q	r	s	t	u	v	w	x	y	z	a	b	c	d	e	F
G	g	h	i	j	k	l	m	n	o	p	q	r	s	t	u	v	w	x	y	z	a	b	c	d	e	f	G
H	h	i	j	k	l	m	n	o	p	q	r	s	t	u	v	w	x	y	z	a	b	c	d	e	f	g	H
I	i	j	k	l	m	n	o	p	q	r	s	t	u	v	w	x	y	z	a	b	c	d	e	f	g	h	I
J	j	k	l	m	n	o	p	q	r	s	t	u	v	w	x	y	z	a	b	c	d	e	f	g	h	i	J
K	k	l	m	n	o	p	q	r	s	t	u	v	w	x	y	z	a	b	c	d	e	f	g	h	i	j	K
L	l	m	n	o	p	q	r	s	t	u	v	w	x	y	z	a	b	c	d	e	f	g	h	i	j	k	L
M	m	n	o	p	q	r	s	t	u	v	w	x	y	z	a	b	c	d	e	f	g	h	i	j	k	l	M
N	n	o	p	q	r	s	t	u	v	w	x	y	z	a	b	c	d	e	f	g	h	i	j	k	l	m	N
O	o	p	q	r	s	t	u	v	w	x	y	z	a	b	c	d	e	f	g	h	i	j	k	l	m	n	O
P	p	q	r	s	t	u	v	w	x	y	z	a	b	c	d	e	f	g	h	i	j	k	l	m	n	o	P
Q	q	r	s	t	u	v	w	x	y	z	a	b	c	d	e	f	g	h	i	j	k	l	m	n	o	p	Q
R	r	s	t	u	v	w	x	y	z	a	b	c	d	e	f	g	h	i	j	k	l	m	n	o	p	q	R
S	s	t	u	v	w	x	y	z	a	b	c	d	e	f	g	h	i	j	k	l	m	n	o	p	q	r	S
T	t	u	v	w	x	y	z	a	b	c	d	e	f	g	h	i	j	k	l	m	n	o	p	q	r	s	T
U	u	v	w	x	y	z	a	b	c	d	e	f	g	h	i	j	k	l	m	n	o	p	q	r	s	t	U
V	v	w	x	y	z	a	b	c	d	e	f	g	h	i	j	k	l	m	n	o	p	q	r	s	t	u	V
W	w	x	y	z	a	b	c	d	e	f	g	h	i	j	k	l	m	n	o	p	q	r	s	t	u	v	W
X	x	y	z	a	b	c	d	e	f	g	h	i	j	k	l	m	n	o	p	q	r	s	t	u	v	w	X
Y	y	z	a	b	c	d	e	f	g	h	i	j	k	l	m	n	o	p	q	r	s	t	u	v	w	x	Y
Z	z	a	b	c	d	e	f	g	h	i	j	k	l	m	n	o	p	q	r	s	t	u	v	w	x	y	Z
	A	B	C	D	E	F	G	H	I	J	K	L	M	N	O	P	Q	R	S	T	U	V	W	X	Y	Z	

To encrypt or decipher a Vigenére cipher, both the sender and the receiver must know a key word. Carroll chose the word VIGILANCE. This is how a message would be encrypted:

1. Choose a key word—any word you want. (We will work here with Lewis Carroll's word.)

2. Write your message: COME QUICKLY NEED SUPPLIES

3. Write the letters of the key word above each letter in the message.

```
V I G I L A N C E V I G I L A N C E V I G I L
C O M E Q U I C K L Y N E E D S U P P L I E S
```

4. Use the Vigenére Table to encode the cipher. The first letter of the message is C with the letter V above it. Find the intersection of the V column and the C row on the Vigenére Table. It is x. The first letter of the cipher is x. The second letter of the message is O with an I above it. On the matrix, the I column intersects with the O row at w; therefore, w is the second letter. The third letter of the cipher is the G column, and the M row; fourth letter is I column, E row, and so forth. This is how the enciphering looks:

```
V I G I L A N C E V I G I L A N C E V I G I L
C O M E Q U I C K L Y N E E D S U P P L I E S
x w s m b u v e o g g t m p d f w t k t o m d
```

5. Place the letters in groups of four or five.

```
xwsmb uveog gtmpd fwtkt omdur
```

The final two letters are called nulls.

6. The receiver of the message must know the key word. When he receives the enciphered message, he writes the letters of the key word above each message letter.

```
V I G I L A N C E V I G I L A N C E V I G I L A N
x w s m b u v e o g g t m p d f w t k t o m d u r
```

7. Decoding is easy now. The first letter is V with an x below it. Go straight down the V column to x. It is in row C; therefore, C is the first letter of the message. Then go down the I column to w. It is in the O row, so the second letter is O. G/s is M, I/m is E, and so on.

Algebraic Codes Using Coordinate Planes

Students who know how to plot points and lines on a coordinate plane can encipher and decipher algebraically. (See pages 85–87 of this text.)

The equation for a line is $y = ax + b$ or, in a simpler form, $y = x + b$. For a cipher, x = letter in, b = some number, y = letter out. Both the sender and the receiver must know the value of b, the key number.

Here is how this system works:

1. Let $b = 6$ (or any other number). Make a table of the coordinates.

If x is	then y is	and the coordinates are
x	$x + 6 = y$	(x, y)
1	$1 + 6 = 7$	$(1, 7)$
2	$2 + 6 = 8$	$(2, 8)$
3	$3 + 6 = 9$	$(3, 9)$
4	$4 + 6 = 10$	$(4, 10)$
5	$5 + 6 = 11$	$(5, 11)$
6	$6 + 6 = 12$	$(6, 12)$

2. Plot the points (or any two points) on the graph. Through these points draw the line $y = x + 6$.

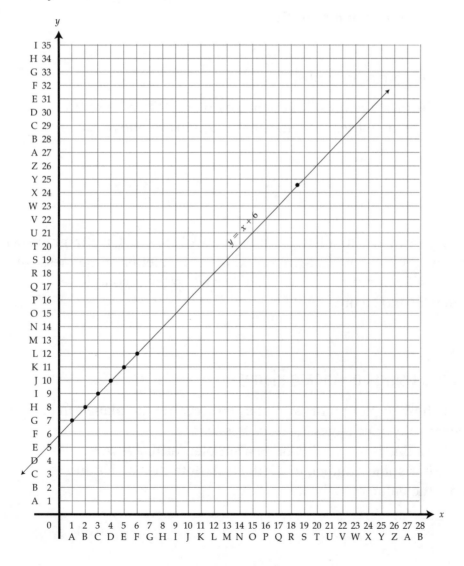

3. To encrypt, find the known letter of the message on the *x*-axis. Find the point on the line which is directly above that letter. What is its coordinate on the *y*-axis? That letter begins the encrypted message.

Example

The message is GOODBYE. Find G on the *x*-axis (7). Move straight up to the point on the line and read across to the *y*-axis to M (13). The first letter of the code is M. The completed encryption is: M U U J H E K

4. Have students create messages for each other choosing different values for *b*. They also may try a more complicated equation such as $y = ax + b$.

If *x* is	then	and *y* is	and the coordinates are
x	$2x + 3$	*y*	(x, y)
0	$2(0) + 3$	3	$(0, 3)$
1	$2(1) + 3$	5	$(1, 5)$
2	$2(2) + 3$	7	$(2, 7)$
3	$2(3) + 3$	9	$(3, 9)$

Graph the points, draw the line, and encrypt the message.

5. Remind students that the receiver must know the key line's equation. However, never send the key with the message. Anyone who intercepts the message could decipher it.

Challenge

In Part VI, Chapter 1, of *Figgs and Phantoms*, Remus sings:

"I'm very well acquainted, too,
    with matters mathematical,
I understand equations,
    both simple and quadratical."

What is the difference between a simple equation and a quadratical one?

[Answer: A simple equation is a linear equation whose graph is a line. It can be written as $y = ax + b$.
A quadratical equation is graphed as a curve—a parabola. Graphing the height and time of a thrown ball would take this shape—up, up, up, then down, down, down. A quadratic equation can be written in the form $ax^2 + bx + c = 0$ when $a \neq 0$.]

For Further Study

Not all codes are written with symbols, letters, and numbers. Other languages have been used for secret messages. For instance, during World War II the United States used an unbreakable code—the Navajo language—to send secret messages to help defeat it enemies.

Suggested Reading on Navajo Code Talkers

Aaseng, Nathan. *Navajo Code Talkers.* New York: Walker and Company, 1992.

Daily, Robert. *The Code Talkers: American Indians in World War II.* New York: Franklin Watts, 1995.

Hunter, Sara Hoagland. *The Unbreakable Code.* Flagstaff, Arizona: Northland Publishing Company, 1996.

Kawano, Kenji. *Warriors: Navajo Code Talkers.* Flagstaff, Arizona: Northland Publishing Company, 1990.

Related Books

Gardner, Martin. *Codes, Ciphers, and Secret Writing.* New York: Simon and Schuster, 1972.

Huckle, Helen. *The Secret Code Book.* New York: Dial Books, 1995.

Kahn, David. *The Codebreakers: The Story of Secret Writing.* New York: Macmillan Publishing Company, 1967.

Pickering, Fran. *Super Secret Code Book.* New York: Sterling Publishing Company, 1995.

Poe, Edgar Allan. *The Gold Bug and Other Tales.* Mineola, New York: Dover, 1991.

Poe, Edgar Allan. *The Gold Bug: Classic Short Story Series.* Mankato, Minnesota: Creative Education Library, 1990.

Poe, Edgar Allan. *The Gold Bug: Illustrated Classics Series.* Chicago: Jamestown Publishers, 1987.

Schwartz, Alvin. *The Cat's Elbow and Other Secret Languages.* New York: Farrar, Straus, and Giroux, 1982.

Smoothey, Marion. *Let's Investigate Graphs.* New York: Marshall Cavendish Corporation, 1995.

Statistics

Graph Types and Uses

In the statistics lessons in this chapter, students will be required to display data on a variety of graphs. Use the following as examples.

Pictograph Compares data.

Zoo Attendance

Thursday	
Friday	
Saturday	
Sunday	

 = 100 people

Bar Graph Compares data.

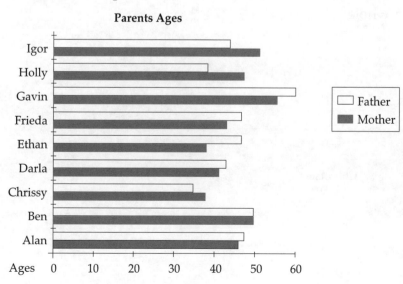

Parents Ages

□ Father
■ Mother

Bar Graph Compares data.

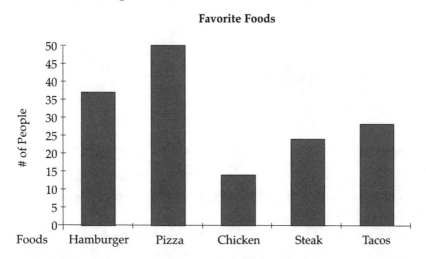

Line Graph Shows changes.

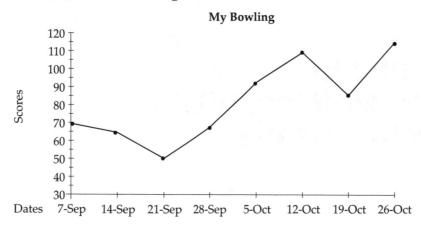

Circle Graph Shows parts of a whole.

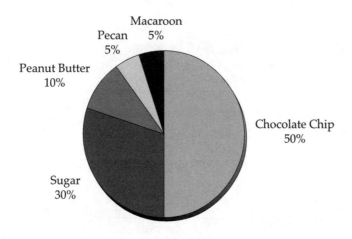

Woodsong

by Gary Paulsen
New York: Bradbury Press, 1990

Gary Paulsen's autobiographical account begins with the story of how he fell in love with his dogs and dog racing in Minnesota, and ends with the story of Paulsen's participation in the Iditarod—the 1000-mile dogsled race across Alaska from Anchorage to Nome.

Dogsong

by Gary Paulsen
New York: Bradbury Press, 1985

A fourteen-year-old Eskimo boy is confused by the clashes of his ancient and modern cultures. To find his own "song," he journeys across 1400 miles of ice, tundra, and mountains by dogsled.

You will decide if the entire class reads the same novel (i.e., *Woodsong* or *Dogsong* in trade books) or if students choose to read their own fiction or nonfiction book about the Iditarod such as the ones listed at the end of this section. Use the books to raise interest in this event. The books themselves are not needed to complete the activities. Necessary information is included here or is gathered by students from newspapers, almanacs, interviews, and so on. Once students have worked through some of these lessons, they (or you) may have ideas on how to display and work with the statistics that are found in each book.

Topics Statistics from the Iditarod and Alaska

Objectives To construct and understand different ways to represent data with graphs and distribution plots and demonstrate understanding of the statistical concepts of range, mean, median, and mode

Applicable NCTM Standards 1, 2, 3, 4, 5, 7, 10

Length of the Iditarod Race

The Iditarod is a 1049-mile sled-dog race across Alaska from Anchorage in the south-central part of the state to Nome on the western shore of the Bering Sea. The race is described as 1049 miles long, but this is a symbolic figure—the 1000 miles is an approximation, and the 49 miles symbolizes that Alaska is the 49th state. The race actually is closer to 1200 miles long.

1. Using a map of your state, figure out a route for a 1200 mile race where you live. If you live in a small state, what strategies can you use?   [circuitous route, zigzag route, crisscrossing route]

Area and Population Comparisons with Pictorial Graphing

Alaska is the largest state in the Union, but it is one of the least populated.

1. On a bulletin board or wall, make pictorial graphs comparing Alaska's area and population to the area and population of other states.

2. Find the area of each state. Figure out a way to represent this information in a highly visual mode. Have students brainstorm ideas and decide on the best way to present the data.   [One idea: Using 1 cm graph paper (see Figure 1.6, page 33), have each square represent 1000 square miles. Alaska's square mileage would be represented by 586 squares; Rhode Island's would be 1.5 squares.]

3. Now figure out a way to represent each state's population with pictographs which can be displayed beside the area data. Total populations, average persons per square mile, or both can be used. Make sure students understand the meaning of the phrase "people per square mile." Use words like these: "It's as if we took all the people in the state, and spread them evenly over the state …" Give the graph a title, clear labels, and a key.

4. Who would ever need to work with this data? Make up five questions from this information that you could ask a partner.

Distances Using Stem-and-Leaf Plots and a Conversion Graph

The route of the race varies from year to year. Hand out copies of Figure 4.1 which shows the distances between checkpoints for an Iditarod race which followed the southern route.

Figure 4.1 Reproducible
Iditarod Checkpoints and Distances

Anchorage to Eagle River	20 miles
Eagle River to Settler's Bay	34 miles
Settler's Bay to Knik	08 miles
Knik to Rabbit Lake	52 miles
Rabbit Lake to Skwentna	34 miles
Skwentna to Finger Lake	45 miles
Finger Lake to Rainy Pass	30 miles
Rainy Pass to Rohn	48 miles
Rohn to Nikolai	90 miles
Nikolai to McGrath	48 miles
McGrath to Takotna	23 miles
Takotna to Ophir	38 miles
Ophir to Iditarod	90 miles
Iditarod to Shageluk	65 miles
Shageluk to Anvik	25 miles
Anvik to Grayling	18 miles
Grayling to Eagle Island	60 miles
Eagle Island to Kaltag	70 miles
Kaltag to Unalakleet	90 miles
Unalakleet to Shaktoolik	40 miles
Shaktoolik to Koyuk	58 miles
Koyuk to Elim	48 miles
Elim to Golovin	28 miles
Golovin to White Mountain	18 miles
White Mountain to Mountain Safety	55 miles
Mountain Safety to Nome	22 miles
Total	**1157 miles**

A stem-and-leaf plot is helpful to organize this type data. In a stem-and-leaf plot, the tens digits are listed vertically as stems and the ones digits are listed horizontally as leaves. For example, the numbers 25, 18, 15, 22, 27 (ordered: 15, 18, 22, 25, 27) would be plotted like this:

Stem	Leaves
1	5 8
2	2 5 7

1. How would the mileages 99, 96, 97, 91, 93, 90, and 97 be plotted?
    [9 | 0 1 3 6 7 7 9]

2. How many miles are represented in the line above?
    [90 + 91 + 93 + 96 + 97 + 97 + 99 = 663 miles]

3. Make a stem-and-leaf plot for the distances between the Iditarod checkpoints in Figure 4.1.

    Answer

Stem	Leaves
0	8
1	8 8
2	0 2 3 5 8
3	0 4 4 8
4	0 5 8 8 8
5	2 5 8
6	0 5
7	0
8	
9	0 0 0

4. Using the stem-and-leaf display created above, answer these questions:

    a. What numbers are shown by the third stem and its leaves?   [20, 22, 23, 25, 28]

    b. What do these numbers represent?   [mileages in the twenties between five sets of towns]

    c. Which mileage occurs more frequently, 34 or 28?   [34]

    d. Which mileage occurs less frequently, 70 or 18?   [70]

5. Find the range of the data.   [The range of a group of numbers is the difference between the greatest and least numbers. It is the measure of the distance between extremes—the last stem-and-leaf minus the first stem-and-leaf: 90 − 8 = 82. The range of the data is 82.]

6. Find the median of the data.   [The median is the number that is located in the center of the data. There are 26 leaves, so the median is located between the first 13 and the last 13. In this case the center is between 40 and 45, so the median is 42.5.]

7. What is the mode?   [It is the number that appears most frequently. Both 48 and 90 occur three times, so this data has two modes. It is bimodal.]

Miles Versus Kilometers

Use the list of distances in Figure 4.1, page 111, and the miles/kilometers conversion graph, Figure 4.2, page 114, to answer the following questions:

1. A distance of 60 miles is about how many kilometers?   [96 kilometers]

2. A distance of 60 kilometers is about how many miles?   [about 37 or 38 miles]

3. Which is longer, a mile or a kilometer?   [a mile]

4. About how many kilometers is it from Rohn to Nikolai?   [about 143 or 144 kilometers]

5. About how many kilometers is it from Iditarod to Shagaluk?   [about 104 kilometers]

6. When a racer gets to Golovin, how many miles does he have to go to the finish line?   [95 mi.]   About how many kilometers is that?   [about 151 or 152 kilometers]

7. Using the data below, and without doing any written calculation, quickly estimate the length of the Iditarod in kilometers.   [for a 1000 mile race, 1600 kilometers]

   - 1 mile ≈ 1.6 kilometers

   - 10 miles ≈ 16 kilometers

   - 100 miles ≈ 160 kilometers

Mean Distances—Average as a Statistical Idea

It takes most racers between two and three weeks to finish the Iditarod. The record was set by Doug Swingley from Simms, Montana, who finished in 9 days, 2 hours, 42 minutes, and 19 seconds.

1. Round Doug Swingley's time to the nearest day, and figure out about how far he had to travel each day to keep this pace. (In other words, determine his mean pace.)   [1200 ÷ 9 = 133.33; more than 133 miles a day]

Figure 4.2 Reproducible
Relationship Between Miles and Kilometers

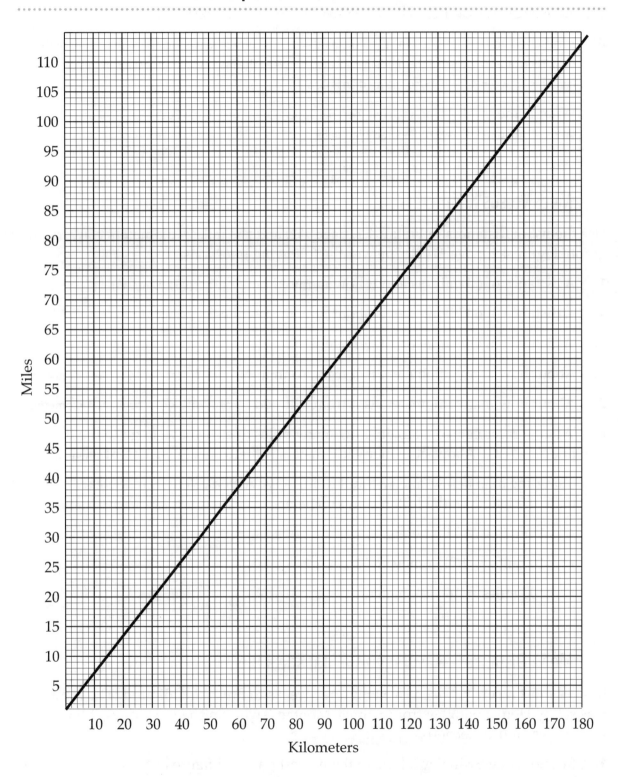

2. Actually, each racer is required to take a 24-hour rest stop. Now figure his mean pace.   [1200 ÷ 8 = 150 miles a day]

3. Make up a mileage log for Doug that would give this mean.

Example

Day 1	154 miles
Day 2	138 miles
Day 3	158 miles
Day 4	149 miles

And so on.

Note Use this exercise to determine if students understand average as a statistical idea. To find an average (median) they generally are accustomed to adding a column of figures and dividing by the number of data in the set without understanding the concept of average. Some students can construct the data by creating a symmetrical distribution: mileages of 149 and 151, then 148 and 152, 147, 153, and so on. Some might try patterns of 145, 145, 145, ... 155, 155, 155, and so forth. Introduce a constraint which would not allow them to make a symmetrical distribution.

Graphing Temperatures and Making Inferences

The Iditarod sled-dog racers travel over some of the most treacherous and beautiful terrain in the world. They race through jagged mountain ranges, over frozen rivers, through dense forests, on desolate tundra, and along miles of windswept coasts. They fight temperatures that can fall to −60° F (−100° F with the wind chill) and winds that can cause complete loss of vision. They contend with wild animals and long hours of darkness.

1. Are the temperatures of Anchorage and Nome listed daily in your newspaper? If not, use Anchorage and another city in Alaska. Collect this data for the month of March and graph it. Record each day's temperature.

2. For a similar or alternative activity, use the actual temperatures along the route. Some personal accounts, such as *Race Across Alaska* by Libby Riddles (1988), record each day's temperature.

3. Determine with the class what kind of graph will communicate this data most clearly.   [line graph]

a. What is the graph's title?   [Sample answer: Daily Temperatures During the Itidarod]

b. What will the horizontal axis be labeled?   [Sample answer: Days of the Race]

c. What will the vertical axis be labeled?   [Sample answer: Temperature]

4. How can you record data from two cities on one graph?   [Use a different color line for each city. This must be explained in a key at the bottom of the graph.]   Who would ever need to know this information? Why?

5. Write three things you can infer from this data. For instance, are temperatures always lower at higher latitudes?

6. Why are the temperatures on Alaska's coasts sometimes warmer than those on the interior of the state?   [Sample answer: The ocean provides a moderating effect.]

7. Using this data, write five questions that you can ask a partner.

Graphing Ethnic Distributions and Making Inferences

Iditarod racers come not only from Alaska but from all over the United States and other countries. Many ethnic groups are represented. Using an almanac, find out what groups of people make up Alaska's population and graph it.

1. What kind of graph will communicate this data most clearly?   [circle graph]

2. Before you begin, draw a circle and show approximately how you think the graph will be divided. Estimate. Later, compare this to your finished circle graph.

3. Draw your graph according to the following steps:

    a. Round each ethnic group's percentage to the nearest whole number.

    b. Write each percentage as a decimal fraction.

    c. Multiply each decimal by 360° (because there are 360° in a circle) to determine how many degrees it will take up in the circle.

    Example

    • 15.6% of Alaskans are American Indian, Aleut, or Eskimo.

    • Round.   [16%]

    • Convert to decimal.   [.16]

    • Multiply by 360°   [.16 × 360° = 57.6° ≈ 58°]

    • This group will take up 58° of the circle.

    d. Use a compass to draw a circle.

e. Draw one radius.

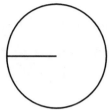

f. Place the center of the protractor's base on the center of the circle and place the edge on the radius.

g. Draw a 58° angle.

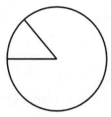

h. Place the protractor on the new radius and draw the angle of the next group. Continue.

i. Title and label the graph.

3. Follow the same procedure for your state's population.

4. Collect ethnicity data for your own school (or school district). Does your school's ethnic distribution look like your state's? Why?

Distributing Expenses

Mushers usually need between $25,000 and $30,000 to race. They pay a $1249 entrance fee, and then they have added expenses for their dog team, food supplies, and equipment.

The first twenty racers who cross the finish line receive cash prizes. The winner gets $50,000, with the amounts decreasing down to $4500. Additionally, the mushers who come in between 21st and 60th receive $1000 each. In 1991 the first twenty finishers were paid a total of $300,000.

1. Figure out a way this money could have been paid out and graph it. Use a computer to graph the information in as many ways as you can think of. Which way conveys the data most clearly?

2. The Iditarod's annual budget is about $1,700,000. Brainstorm ideas for all the things this money is spent on.

3. If 60 people enter the Iditarod, about how much does the race cost per person? [$28,333]

4. Some people race year after year without winning any money. Why do you suppose they do this?

5. What lessons about life do the racers learn?

Related Books

The Alaska Almanac: Facts About Alaska. Anchorage: Alaska Northwest Books, published yearly, [Brochure].

Calvert, Patricia. *The Hour of the Wolf.* New York: Charles Scribner's Sons, 1983.

Cooper, Michael. *Racing Sled Dogs: An Original North American Sport.* New York: Clarion Books, 1988.

Crisman, Ruth. *Racing the Iditarod Trail.* New York: Dillon Press, 1993.

Dolan, Ellen M. *Susan Butcher and the Iditarod Trail.* New York: Walker and Company, 1993.

Jones, Tim. *The Last Great Race: The Iditarod.* Harrisburg, Pennsylvania: Stackpole Books, 1988.

O'Dell, Scott. *Black Star, Bright Dawn.* Boston: Houghton Mifflin Company, 1988.

Paulsen, Gary. *Winterdance: The Fine Madness of Running the Iditarod.* New York: Harcourt Brace & Company, 1994.

Riddles, Libby and Tim Jones. *Race Across Alaska: The First Woman to Win the Iditarod Tells Her Story.* Harrisburg, Pennsylvania: Stackpole Books, 1988.

Wadsworth, Ginger. *Susan Butcher: Sled Dog Racer.* Minneapolis, Minnesota: Lerner Publications Company, 1994.

In the Year of the Boar and Jackie Robinson

by Bette Bao Lord

New York: Harper & Row, Publishers, 1984

A Chinese girl, who renames herself Shirley Temple Wong, comes to Brooklyn, New York, in 1947. She does not feel at home until she discovers baseball, the Brooklyn Dodgers, and Jackie Robinson.

This book is appropriate for students in grades 3–7 and can be taught on any level. It is available as a trade book and also as part of purchasable Read Aloud and/or Literature Units:

- Developmental Studies Center Staff. *In the Year of the Boar and Jackie Robinson: Read Aloud Unit*, 1996.

- Nakajima, Caroline. *In the Year of the Boar and Jackie Robinson: Study Guide.* Teacher Created Materials, 1992.

- Tretter, Marcia. *In the Year of the Boar and Jackie Robinson: Children's Literature Unit.* Learning Links, 1988.

Yang the Youngest and His Terrible Ear

by Lensey Namioka
Boston: Little, Brown and Company, 1992

Yang Yingtao and his family move from China to Seattle. Everyone in the family is musically talented except Yang. Because he is tone-deaf, he does not feel like he fits in the family. In fact, he would rather be playing baseball.

This book is appropriate for students in grades 3–7 and can be taught on any level. It is available as a trade book and also as part of purchasable Read Aloud and/or Literature Units:

- Developmental Studies Center Staff. *Yang the Youngest and His Terrible Ear: Read Aloud Unit*, 1996.

- Ferraro, Bonnie. *Yang the Youngest and His Terrible Ear: Children's Literature Unit.* Learning Links, 1995.

Topics Immigrants, minorities, and baseball

Objective To work with statistics in a variety of fields, including grass-covered ones

Applicable NCTM Standards 1, 2, 3, 4, 5, 7, 9, 10, 11

Using Charts to Organize Data from Literature

We use charts, graphs, and tables to organize information and to display it in a manner that makes it easy to read and to work with. Charting can be used with literature to achieve those same purposes.

1. Use a chart to organize topics and thoughts as a prewriting tool for a comparison/contrast essay on the books *In the Year of the Boar and Jackie Robinson* and *Yang the Youngest and His Terrible Ear.*

Example

Comparison/Contrast Chart

Topic	Similarities	Differences
Setting		
Urban setting		
Ethnic makeup of neighborhood		
Plot		
The story line		
Main characters		
Ways they are accepted or rejected		
Their best friends		
Culture of homeland/American culture		
Home life		
Roles of Women		
Attitudes toward		

- Family

- School

- Sports

- Music

- Priorities concerning earning/ spending money

- Accepting compliments

Ways baseball influenced their lives

- This chart is used as a prewriting tool to organize students' thoughts and information. To keep the theme focused, the chart should be entitled with whatever the student has chosen for a controlling idea.

- The controlling idea is repeated in both the introduction and the concluding paragraph.

- Paragraphing is simplified because the main topics are already divided.

- Topic sentences can be constructed around the topic phrases in the first column.

- Transition words, phrases, or sentences at the beginning of each paragraph keep the essay flowing as a solid whole.

- Some students may have so much information recorded under one topic—main characters or cultural differences, for instance—that they may wish to write the entire essay on that narrower topic.

- The chart is just the first step in the process of completing and handing in a detailed, well-written essay.

Immigration Statistics

The United States is a nation inhabited by immigrants. Shirley Temple Wong's family emigrated here about 35 years before Yang's. Immigration records have been kept only since 1820. Give each student a copy of the immigration graph, Figure 4.3, to practice interpreting graphs while answering the questions posed in Figure 4.4 in a group discussion. Or for independent work, give each student a copy of the questions.

Answers to Figure 4.4

1. years—the first, 1880; the second, 1980; 2. 1600 thousands, interpreted correctly as 1,600,000 or 1.6 million people; 3. answers will vary; 4. Shirley Temple Wong—1947, Yang Yingtao—recently, use your own judgment; 5. 75,000 in 1947 and perhaps 1,100,000 in recent years; 6. the Civil War; 8. answers will vary; 9. answers will vary; 10. 1830s; 11. answers will vary; 12. The 1986 amnesty program combined with the loosened restriction of immigration laws in 1990.

We Are All Immigrants

1. Have your class tally the national origins of the students. If someone is Dutch/Scotch/Irish, give the Netherlands, Scotland, and Ireland each a tally mark.

2. What kind of graph would best display this data? Construct the graph and hang it in your classroom.

Figure 4.3 Reproducible
Immigrants Admitted: 1820–1991

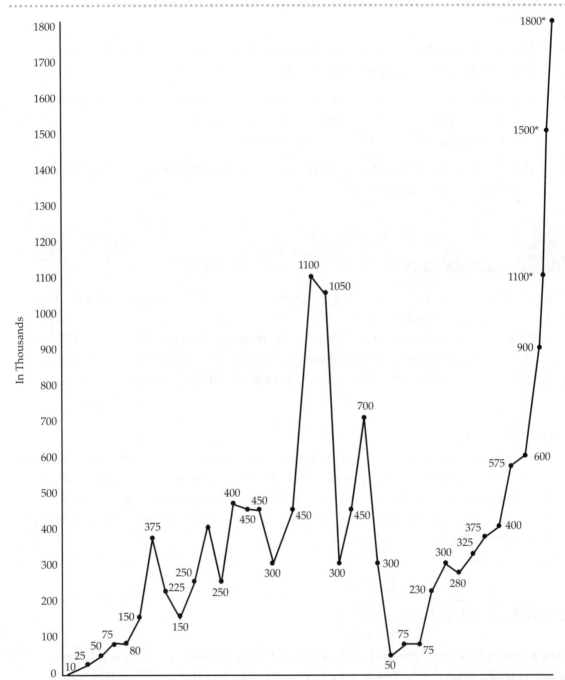

*Includes amnestied applicants

Source: Immigration and Naturalization Service

1989-500,000   1990-900,000   1991-1,100,000

Graph from *The Challenge of Immigration* by Vic Cox (1995) used by permission of Enslow Publishers, Inc.

Figure 4.4 Reproducible
Immigration Statistics

1. Two 80s are listed on the horizontal axis. What do they represent?

2. Find 1600 on the vertical axis. What does it represent?

3. In the year you were born, about how many immigrants were admitted to the United States?

4. Both of the main characters in *In the Year of the Boar and Jackie Robinson* and *Yang the Youngest and His Terrible Ear* are immigrants from China. In about what years did they emigrate?

5. About how many other immigrants were admitted to the United States in those years?

6. Look at the drop in immigration at the beginning of the 1860s. What was happening in the United States at that time? Why would people not come here then?

7. How do you explain the huge increase in the number of immigrants at the beginning of the century?

8. What caused the decline of immigration in the 1930s? What is the historical significance of the low immigration numbers in the 1930s and 1940s?

9. The number of immigrants in the 1930s and 1940s is about the same as what other years?

10. What is the immigration trend from the 1950s on? How do you explain this? What are the social implications for the United States? That is, what is happening in our society because of these increased numbers of immigrants? (Be sure to look for positive effects as well as negative ones.)

11. From your immigration research, explain the dramatic increase in immigration since 1985.

12. Find books to read about immigration and immigrants like *The Challenge of Immigration* by Vic Cox (1995). Others are listed in the Related Books at the end of the section.

3. The next data will be a little harder to collect; it might take some family research. What year(s) did your family come to America? Native Americans can find when their ancient ancestors crossed into North America from Asia by the Bering Strait.

4. Make a graph of your classroom data similar to the immigration graph show in Figure 4.3. Are there any similarities in the graphs?

5. What would happen if you increased the size of the group you questioned— your sample population? Expand the sample population (the whole school? a few members of each class?). Graph the new data. What has changed? Why?

6. What size sample population would you need to get data that resembles that shown in Figure 4.3? Why?

Baseball—A Reflection of Our Culture?

1. In *In the Year of the Boar and Jackie Robinson*, how does Shirley Temple Wong's teacher, Mrs. Rappaport, compare the game of baseball to life in America? Read her inspiring speech on page 92 and explain it in your own words.

2. Jackie Robinson was the first African-American to play for a major league baseball team. What does Mrs. Rappaport say about his opportunity? Read the passage on page 93 and explain it in your own words.

3. Not all immigrants have come to America willingly. Compare the experience of Africans who came as slaves with that of other ethnic groups.

4. Read books about the struggles that African-Americans went through to play baseball. Some nonfiction books about the Negro Baseball Leagues are listed in Related Books at the end of this section.

5. Read a book about Jackie Robinson. An excellent one is *The Importance of Jackie Robinson* by Arthur Diamond (1992). After White Americans slowly recognized Robinson as an equal ballplayer, they slowly started to see that African-Americans are equal in all areas. This was just the beginning of a major social change in America—an important step in the civil rights movement. Why was Jackie Robinson an excellent choice for this awesome responsibility?

6. In what other ways does baseball reflect what is going on socially in the United States?   [For instance, in the early 1900s social service organizations immersed immigrant youths in baseball as a means of "Americanizing" them. This is how the American Legion got involved in baseball. For a look at how baseball reflects modern cultural attitudes toward drugs, violence, cheating, race discrimination, sex discrimination, and money, see the juvenile nonfiction book by Nathan Aaseng, *The Locker Room Mirror: How Sports Reflect Society* (1993).

7. These are the countries from which major league baseball players have come:

Australia	Denmark	Ireland	Poland
Austria	Dominican Republic	Italy	Russia
Austria-Hungary	England	Japan	Scotland
The Bahamas	Finland	Jamaica	Spain
Canada	France	Mexico	Sweden
China	Germany	Nicaragua	Switzerland
Columbia	Greece	Norway	Venezuela
Cuba	Holland	Okinawa	Wales
Czechoslovakia	Honduras	Panama	

8. Is the country of your family origin listed? If not, why do you think no baseball players have come from there?

9. More players have come from the Dominican Republic and Cuba than all the other nations combined. How do you explain this?

Figuring Baseball Batting Averages

Jackie Robinson's lifetime batting average was .311. That means for every 1000 at bats, he got 311 hits. Different ways of noting this are:

- 311 hits for 1000 at bats

- 311:1000

- $\dfrac{311}{1000}$

- or, as a baseball statistic— .311, which is read "three eleven"

The batting average is the percentage of hits per times at bat. This is sometimes abbreviated Avg. or Pct. In this statistic, "at bat" does not mean every time the batter steps up to the plate. If he sacrifices (purposely hits a ball that he knows will be caught just so a runner on base can advance to the next base), if he gets a walk, or if he is hit by a pitch, no at bat is counted. So if a player gets up to the plate four times during a game, gets a single base hit, walks twice, and hits a sacrifice, he has only one hit for one at bat in the game. You could say: 1 hit for one at bat, 1:1, $\frac{1}{1}$, 1.000 ÷ 1, or, as a baseball statistic—1.000 (read "one thousand").

Collect Your Own Data

1. Have students take turns taking shots at a wastebasket. Use soft foam balls or even wadded sheets of paper.

2. Have students record the ratio of how many "hits" (baskets) they get compared to how many tries.

    Examples

    *   4 hits for 8 tries is 4 : 8. In sports we say, "four for eight."

        $4 : 8 = \frac{4}{8} = .500$, "five hundred"

    *   3 for 7 = 3 : 7 = $\frac{3}{7} \approx .429$, or "four twenty-nine"

    Do the division out four places—to the thousandths—and round to the hundredths place ($.4285 \approx .429$).

Practice Figuring Baseball Statistics

1. Find batting averages for these players:

    a. 15 at bats (AB); 3 hits (H)   [.200]

    b. 28 H; 82 AB   [.341]

    c. 206 AB; 96 H   [.466]

    d. 17 H; 87 AB   [.195]

    e. 10 H; 18 AB   [.556]

2. **Ready for a challenge?** The player who bats .300 is considered a great hitter while the player who bats .250 is not. These two players have come to the plate 40 times. How many hits did each player get?

    Answer

    x = unknown number of hits out of 40

    $$\frac{x}{40} = .300$$

    $$\frac{x}{40} = \frac{.300}{1}$$

    $1x = (40).300$ (Cross products are equal)

    $x = 12$

    The .300 batter has 12 hits for 40 at bats.

$$\frac{x}{40} = .250$$

$$\frac{x}{40} = \frac{.250}{1}$$

$1x = (40).250$ (Cross products are equal)

$x = 10$

The .250 batter has 10 hits for 40 at bats.

3. What fraction of hits does a .333 batter get?   [$^{333}/_{1000} \approx \frac{1}{3}$. He hits one-third of the time.]

    a. How is that expressed as a percent?   [$\frac{1}{3} \approx 33\%$]

    b. Can you think of any other activity where you are considered great if you are successful $\frac{1}{3}$ or 33% of the time?

Won/Lost Average

A team's record is determined by finding the ratio of wins to the number of games played. A team which plays 58 games and wins only 15 of them is a team playing .259 ball.

- $15 : 58 = 15/58 = 15 \div 58 \approx .259$, or two fifty-nine

1. All these teams played 61 games. Figure the teams' averages.

    a. 42 W   [$42 : 61 \approx .689$]

    b. 42 L   [$19\,W : 61 \approx .312$]

    c. 35 W   [$35 : 61 \approx .574$]

    d. 39 L   [$22\,W : 61 \approx .361$]

2. A baseball team which wins over half its games is having a winning season. What is the baseball average meaning half?   [.500, because $^{500}/_{1000} = \frac{1}{2}$]

3. Which of the teams in problem 1 are having winning seasons?   [1 and 3]

Some People Really Care About These Things!

The *Hidden Game of Baseball* by John Thorn and Pete Palmer (1984) is out of print, but available in libraries. The book is filled with statistics you probably never have considered. The following examples demonstrate why the field of sports needs people who are good in math, people who work only with statistics—statisticians.

In this book, Branch Rickey figured out a formula working with data to gauge the factors which contribute to a winning or losing team (page 41).

$$\left(\frac{H+BB+HP}{AB+BB+HP}+\frac{3(TB-H)}{4AB}-\frac{R}{H+BB+HP}\right)-\left(\frac{H}{AB}+\frac{BB+HB}{AB+BB-HB}+\frac{ER}{H+BB+HB}-\frac{SO}{8(AB+H+HB)}-F\right)=G$$

Team's Offense (runs scored)   –   Team's Defense (runs allowed)   = G

- In this formula, the variables are baseball statistics which are abbreviated this way:

H	hits
BB	base on balls
HP	hit by pitch
AB	at bats
TB	total bases
R	runs
ER	earned runs
SO	strike outs
F	fielding
G	game

- The formula represents a total game (or games) by its statistical parts.

- The minuend is the team's offense, or runs scored.

- The subtrahend represents the defense, or runs allowed.

- The difference ($-$) between the two shows how efficient the team is.

- If the first part is greater than the second, the team wins.

- G is the won-lost percentage and will be greater than .500 for a winning team.

In working with probabilities, you might have determined things like, What is the probability of getting a 7 on the next roll of the dice? But baseball statisticians want to figure out things like, What is the probability that we can win this game if it is the seventh inning and we are one run behind? They use formulas that look like this (page 155): $Pb \times Vs + (1 - Pb) \times Vf = Vp$.

The math is too difficult for us to do right now, but it is interesting to know that people can (and do!) figure these things out mathematically.

Alone Against the World

1. Remember that Shirley Temple Wong's teacher said that when a baseball player "comes to bat, he stands alone. One man. Many opportunities" (page 92). At any point in a baseball game, the situation is one player against nine players. What does this mean?

2. A batter is at the plate. Explain how he is one player against nine. ("One man, many opportunities.")

3. Describe three different situations that could happen to him. How do your plays compare to other students'?

4. A runner is leading off at second base. How is she one player against nine? Describe three different situations that could happen to her. How do your plays compare to other students'?

Related Books

Immigrant/Minority Baseball, Fiction
Christopher, Matt. *No Arm in Left Field*. Boston: Little, Brown and Company, 1974.
Christopher, Matt. *Shortstop from Mexico*. Boston: Little, Brown and Company, 1988.
Koningsburg, E. L. *About the B'Nai Bagels*. New York: Atheneum, 1971.
Myers, Walter Dean. *Me, Mop, and the Moondance Kid*. New York: Delacorte Press, 1988.
Myers, Walter Dean. *Mop, Moondance, and the Nagasaki Knights*. New York: Delacorte Press, 1992.

Immigrants/Immigration
Ashabranner, Jennifer. *Still a Nation of Immigrants*. New York: Cobblehill Books, 1993.
Cox, Vic. *The Challenge of Immigration*. Springfield, New Jersey: Enslow Publishers, 1995.
Goldish, Meish. *Immigration: How Should It Be Controlled?* New York: Twenty-First Century Books, 1994.
Grenquist, Barbara. *Cubans*. New York: Franklin Watts, 1991.
Reimers, David M. *The Immigrant Experience*. New York: Chelsea House Publishers, 1989.
Sandler, Martin W. *Immigrants*. New York: HarperCollins Publishers, 1995.

Jackie Robinson, Minorities, and Baseball—History
Bergman, Irwin B. *Jackie Robinson: Breaking Baseball's Color Barrier*. New York: Chelsea House Publishers, 1994.

Burns, Ken. Baseball. *The Third Inning: The Faith of Fifty Million People* (Video). PBS Home Video, 1994.

Clark, Dick and Larry Lester, Editors. *The Negro Leagues Book.* Cleveland: The Society for American Baseball Research, 1994.

Cooper, Michael. *Playing America's Game: The Story of Negro League Baseball.* New York: Lodestar Books, 1993.

Diamond, Arthur. *The Importance of Jackie Robinson.* San Diego: Lucent Books, 1992.

Grabowski, John. *Jackie Robinson.* New York: Chelsea House Publishers, 1991.

Greene, Carol. *Jackie Robinson: Baseball's First Black Major-Leaguer.* Chicago: Children's Press, 1990.

Mochizuki, Ken. *Baseball Saved Us.* New York: Lee and Low Books, 1993. (Baseball in Japanese internment camp—World War II)

Rennert, Richard. *Book of Firsts: Sports Heroes.* New York: Chelsea House, 1994.

Press, David P. *A Multicultural Portrait of Professional Sports.* New York: Marshall Cavendish, 1994.

Sanford, William R. and Carl R. Green. *Jackie Robinson.* New York: Crestwood House, 1992.

Ward, Geoffrey C. and Ken Burns. *Shadow Ball: The History of the Negro Leagues.* New York: Alfred A. Knopf, 1994.

Weidhorn, Manfred. *Jackie Robinson.* New York: Atheneum, 1993.

Baseball

Aaseng, Nathan. *The Locker Room Mirror: How Sports Reflect Society.* New York: Walker and Company, 1993.

Aylesworth, Thomas G. *The Kids' World Almanac of Baseball.* New York: World Almanac, 1996.

Seymour, Harold. *Baseball: The People's Game.* New York: Oxford University Press, 1990.

Thorn, John and Pete Palmer. *Hidden Game of Baseball.* Garden City, New Jersey: Doubleday and Company, 1984.

Women and Baseball

Berlage, Gai Ingham. *Women in Baseball: The Forgotten History.* Westport, Connecticut: Praeger Publishers, 1994.

Gregorich, Barbara. *Women at Play: The Story of Women in Baseball.* San Diego: A Harvest Original, Harcourt Brace & Company, 1993.

Johnson, Susan E. *When Women Played Hardball.* Seattle: Seal Press, 1994.

Kindred, Dave. *The Colorado Silver Bullets: The Women Who Go Toe to Toe With the Men.* Atlanta: Longstreet Press, 1995.

Macy, Sue. *A Whole New Ball Game: The Story of the All-American Girls Professional Baseball League.* New York: Henry Holt and Company, 1993.

Levy, Marilyn. *Run for Your Life.* Boston: Houghton Mifflin, 1996. (Fiction—Black women, track)

A Sudden Silence

by Eve Bunting
New York: Fawcett Juniper, 1988

While Bryan and Jesse Harmon are walking home from a party, a hit-and-run driver kills Bryan. Jesse searches to find the drunk driver. See the notes regarding use of this title in the *Binge* description below.

Binge

by Charles Ferry
Rochester, Michigan: Daisy Hill Press, 1992

Binge is a powerful and painful novel about Weldon Yeager, an eighteen-year-old who goes on a drunken binge. When he drives a car, disastrous consequences follow.

Both *A Sudden Silence* and *Binge* are available in trade books and can be read and discussed together as a whole class. Alternatively, students can decide which of the two they will read independently. The books are to be used as a jumping-off place for discussion on the topic of teenage drinking and driving, and as a means of introducing the subjects to take a statistical look at them.

Both books are written for students in the seventh grade and above. However, the material and language are much stronger in *Binge* than in *A Sudden Silence*. Be sure to preview it to see if it is appropriate for your teaching and for your students to read.

Topic Drinking and driving

Objective To work with statistics on teenage drinking, driving, reaction time and braking distances, and blood alcohol levels

Applicable NCTM Standards 2, 4, 8, 10

Teenage Drinking and Driving Statistics

After reading *A Sudden Silence* by Eve Bunting either as a group or individually, discuss how the drunk driver involved could easily have been one of the teens at the party rather than an adult. The driver could also have been Joseph Plum who had been driving drunk the night of the accident and was so intoxicated that he did not know whether or not he had hit someone (pages 71–72).

The drunk driver in *Binge* by Charles Ferry is a teen. Both books are fiction, but the problem of teenage drinking and driving is prevalent and very real.

In the next activities, students will be able to see how widespread and dangerous the practice of driving drunk is as they collect recent statistics.

Data Collection Through Research and Surveys

1. In order for students to obtain the most up-to-date statistics, teach them how to use research tools such as the *Reader's Guide to Periodical Literature* and newspaper indexes to find recently published articles and information. (Search the topics: Drinking/Driving, Teenage)

2. Students should find and graph these statistics relating to teens. (See pages 116–117 for instructions on making a circle graph.)

   a. The leading causes of death in teenagers:

      - Motor vehicle crashes—42%

      - Other injuries—36%

      - Cancer—6%

      - Heart disease—3%

      - Other diseases—13%

   b. Young people aged 16–24 make up 22% of all drivers, but they cause 44% of all drunk- and drug-related driving accidents.

   c. Every 23 minutes, one person in the U.S. dies in a drunk- or drug-related driving accident.

   d. With the exception of teenagers, death rates in all age groups are dropping. Because of drinking-while-driving accidents, the teen death rate has increased in the past 20 years.

3. An excellent resource book for overview, research, and statistics is *Coping With Drinking and Driving* by Janet Grosshandler (1994).

4. Have students take surveys of all the 16- to 20-year-olds they know to collect, compile, and graph data from questions such as these:

    a. Do you drink alcohol?

    b. Have you ever driven a car after drinking?

5. *Coping With Drinking and Driving* contains an opinion survey on the first two pages containing such statements as:

    • "Some people drive more cautiously after they've been drinking."

    • "If someone you hardly know at a party wants to drive drunk, it's really none of your business."

    • "Alcohol starts affecting you as soon as it is swallowed."

    Students respond with strongly disagree, moderately disagree, unsure, moderately agree, or strongly agree. This survey can be done in class and used as a basis for discussion, or students can use these statements to survey other students' opinions. Results can then be compiled and graphed.

Braking Distance

In *A Sudden Silence*, the driver who hit Bry was so drunk that either her vision was impaired and she did not see him, or her reactions were so slowed by the alcohol that she did not begin to brake until after she hit him. In *Binge*, Weldon saw something in the road, began to brake, but still hit four people walking.

How Much Time Does It Take to Stop a Car?

Hand out copies of Figure 4.5, Stopping Distances. Read or paraphrase the following introduction:

> The time it takes to stop a car is your reaction distance added to your braking distance. This is what reaction distance means: Your eyes see something ahead in the road and send a message to your brain. Your brain sends a message back to your body to stop the car. Your leg muscles step on the break. All that happens in ¾ second. The faster you are going, the more distance you travel in ¾ second. Your car does not stop immediately but continues to travel as you continue pressing on the brakes. The faster you are going, the more distance you travel before stopping.

**Figure 4.5 Reproducible
Stopping Distances**

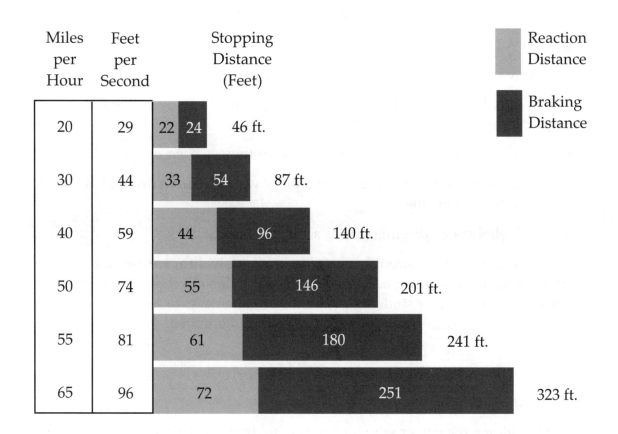

Miles per Hour	Feet per Second	Stopping Distance (Feet)		
20	29	22	24	46 ft.
30	44	33	54	87 ft.
40	59	44	96	140 ft.
50	74	55	146	201 ft.
55	81	61	180	241 ft.
65	96	72	251	323 ft.

Reaction Distance

Braking Distance

1. A car traveling 20 miles per hour is covering 29 feet each second. A car traveling 50 mph is covering how many feet per second?   [74]

2. If you are driving 40 mph, how far will you travel between the time you see something ahead and the time you step on the brakes (reaction distance)? [44 feet]

3. Traveling at 65 mph, how far do you travel between the time you see a hazard ahead and the time you stop?   [323 feet]

4. Find these patterns on the chart:

    a. What is the pattern in the feet per second column?   [For every 10 mph increase, feet per second increase by 15.]

    b. How many feet per second does a car traveling 60 mph go?   [89]

    c. What is the pattern in the reaction column?   [For every 10 mph increase, the reaction distance increases 11 feet.]

    d. What is the reaction distance at 70 mph?   [77 feet]

    e. The pattern in the breaking column is not perfect. What is it?   [Add 30 feet, add about 40 feet, add about 50 feet, about 60 feet, etc.]

    f. What is the approximate braking distance while traveling 60 mph?   [206 feet]

    g. Do you know anything that is about 300 feet long?   [a football field]   What does this statement mean: "Whenever I drive a car 60 miles per hour it is as if I am driving a vehicle that is over 300 feet long. Anything that gets in front of me within that range is going to get hurt."

5. Many textbooks and teachers use questions such as the one Jesse flashes back on in *A Sudden Silence:* "Now students, let's consider question number 32: If a car is approaching from the rear at seventy miles an hour and there is a distance of ..." (page 4).

    a. If you work on this type question, make sure you take your students outside so they can discover and visualize stopping distances. If a car is traveling 50 mph, it needs about 140 feet to stop. That is like half a football field. How long is the block your school is on? Would they ever need that distance to stop? How about half a block?

    b. Also, stress that these stopping distances are under good road conditions and with alert drivers. If the roads are wet or icy they need more time and distance to stop. People who have been drinking have much slower reaction times, so they travel greater distances before applying the brakes.

Blood Alcohol Levels

Some students, especially those closest to driving ages, may be interested in researching, compiling, and displaying statistics related to blood-alcohol levels, impaired reaction times, and the legal consequences of drinking while impaired or drunk.

Culminating Activity: Create Public Service Announcements

1. Divide the students into groups of three or four. Instruct each group to create a 60-second public service announcement about the hazards of teenage drinking and driving.

2. Have students back up thier announcement with graphics—statistical information presented in accurate, large, and easy-to-read graphs, tables, or charts.

3. Make presentations in class, at an assembly or parent program, or even as actual public service announcements aired on a local television station.

Related Books

Diamond, Arthur. *Alcoholism.* San Diego: Lucent Books, 1992.

Grosshandler, Janet. *Coping With Drinking and Driving.* New York: The Rosen Publishing Group, 1994.

Grosshandler, Janet. *Drugs and Driving.* New York: The Rosen Publishing Group, 1992.

Reader's Guide to Periodical Literature. New York: H. W. Wilson Company, semi-monthly.

Your state's drivers' manual.

5

Geometry

If I Were in Charge of the World and Other Worries "Sometimes Poems"

by Judith Viorst
New York: Atheum, 1981

This is a collection of Judith Viorst's poetry for children. On pages 36–37, "Sometimes Poems" begins with a verse in the shape of a trapezoid, changes to a verse resembling a long thin rectangle, and ends with a verse in the form of a line segment.

Topic Linking math and poetry

Objectives To write poetry in various geometric forms and to recognize and classify poetry by metrical patterns

Applicable NCTM Standards 4, 8, 12

Visualizing and Representing Geometric Figures in Poetry

1. Display "Sometimes Poems" from Judith Vorst's book so that everyone can see it, or show the poem on an opaque projector as you read it to the students.

2. Ask students to write poems in different geometric shapes. Even better, have them write poems that are related to the shapes.

Example

Hive and Go Seek

We search for

Hives of six-sided cells,

Hexagon pockets of nectar sweet.

A wax home where a queen dwells

We want to find to eat

Or sell for money.

We seek honey.

Recognizing Poetic Form: Sonnets

Older students should begin to recognize traditional poetry by its form. For instance, all sonnets have fourteen lines and a definite rhyme scheme and meter.

1. Introduce a few poetry terms by their etymologies:

    *   couplet [Fr. *couple*, two]: Two successive lines of poetry that rhyme

    *   quatrain [Fr. *quatre* , l. *quattuor*, four]: A stanza or poem of four lines

    *   sestet [Fr. *sesto*, sixth l. *sextus*, sixth l. *sex*, six]: A stanza or poem of six lines

    *   octave [L. *octavo*, eighth L. *octo*, eight]: A group of eight lines of verse

2. Sonnets can be Petrarchan (Italian) or Shakespearean (English):

    *   A Petrarchan sonnet consists of an octave (two quatrains) with the rhyme scheme abba abba and a sestet with the rhyme scheme either cdc cdc, or cde dce.

    *   A Shakespearean sonnet is arranged with three quatrains and a couplet with the rhyme scheme: abab cdcd efef gg.

3. Have students identify the parts and rhyme scheme of the following poems

    She Used to Let Her Golden Hair Fly Free

    She used to let her golden hair fly free
    For the wind to toy and tangle and molest;
    Her eyes were brighter than the radiant west.
    (Seldom they shine so now.) I used to see

Pity look out of those deep eyes on me.
("It was false pity," you would now protest.)
I had love's tinder heaped within my breast;
What wonder that the flame burned furiously?

She did not walk in any mortal way,
But with angelic progress; when she spoke,
Unearthly voices sang in unison.

She seemed divine among the dreary folk
Of earth. You say she is not so today?
Well, though the bow's unbent, the wound bleeds on.

Francis Petrarch (1304–1374)

No Longer Mourn for Me When I Am Dead

No longer mourn for me when I am dead
Than you shall hear the surly sullen bell
Give warning to the world that I am fled
From this vile world, with vilest worms to dwell:
Nay, if you read this line, remember not
That hand that writ it; for I love you so,
That I in your sweet thoughts would be forgot,
If thinking on me then should make you woe.
O, if, I say, you look upon this verse
When I perhaps compounded am with clay,
Do not so much as my poor name rehearse,
But let your love even with my life decay;
    Lest the wise world should look into your moan,
    And mock with me after I am gone.

(Sonnet LXXI)
William Shakespeare (1564–1616)

4. Build vocabulary based on Greek etymologies while teaching meter.

  • *iambos*   two-syllables—the first unaccented, the second accented as in: iamb'

  • *penta*   five

  • *meter*   measure

  • Iambic pentameter means measuring five two-syllable feet. For instance, "To strive', to seek', to find', and not' to yield'."

5. Have students mark the above poems with accents to find iambic pentameter.

Arrow to the Sun

by Gerald McDermott
New York: The Viking Press, 1974

This book is the retelling of an ancient Pueblo Indian tale richly illustrated with Southwest artwork. A boy searches for his father, endures many trials, and returns to his people.

Topics Recognizing and reproducing symmetrical figures

Objective To recognize and differentiate between different kinds of symmetry in artwork

Applicable NCTM Standards 4, 8, 12

Recognizing Symmetry

1. Hand out copies of Figures 5.1 and 5.2, pages 141–142 so students can practice recognizing and drawing symmetrical figures.

2. If multiple copies of Gerald McDermott's book *Arrow to the Sun* are available, students may work in small groups. For whole group work, pages can be projected with an opaque projector.

3. Read the book aloud to the students making sure to show each page. If you have the audiocassette of the story, play it instead. It is an excellent narration. (McDermott, Gerald. *Arrow to the Sun.* Weston Woods, 1975.)

4. Beginning with the cover and front pages, go through the book again having students find examples of symmetry—reflection, translation, and rotation—in the artwork. If they have Figure 5.1 in front of them, it will help them identify the different types. Then have them reproduce examples of each kind on graph or grid paper (Figure 1.6, page 33).

Figure 5.1 Reproducible
Symmetry

One kind of symmetry is called **reflection.** A mirror set up on the line of symmetry would reflect the image exactly. A reflection also could be flipped over the line of symmetry, and it would fit exactly.

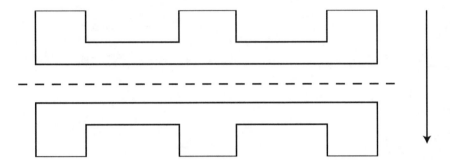

Another kind of symmetry is called **translation.** The figure can be slid along straight lines—right, left, up, down, or a combination of these.

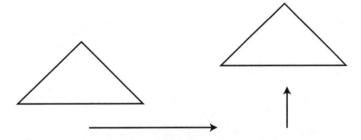

A figure turned around a point is called **rotation** symmetry.

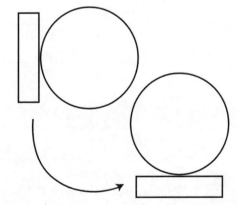

Figure 5.2 Reproducible
Symmetry Practice

Directions For each figure draw a reflection, a translation, and a rotation.

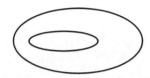

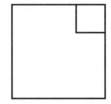

5. Have students read other tales of Southwest cultures. See Related Books below. At your library check for books under subjects such as Navajo Indians Folklore and Mexican Folklore. Although it is now out of print, check the library for *Halo of the Sun: Stories Told and Retold* by Noël Bennett (1987). Bennett describes the sacred act of storytelling and retells Navajo tales, some illustrated with woven baskets and rugs.

6. All ancient tales are retellings of an original story. Writers may read or hear three or more variants of the same story before they write the tale in their own words and style. Have students choose an ancient Southwest Indian story and read it at least three times until they know it well. If possible, they should also read another version of it.

7. Now have the students retell the tale in writing.

8. For the final copy, students illustrate or border the pages with reflectional, rotational, and translational symmetry artwork typical of the culture.

Related Books

Bennett, Noël. *Halo of the Sun: Stories Told and Retold.* Flagstaff, Arizona: Northland Press, 1987.

Bierhorst, John. *The Mythology of Mexico and Central America.* New York: William Morrow and Company, 1990.

Bruchac, Joseph and Gayle Ross. *The Girl Who Married the Moon: Stories From Native North America.* Mahwah, N.J.: BridgeWater Books, 1994.

Cunningham, Keith. *American Indians' Kitchen-Table Stories.* Little Rock, Arkansas: August House Publishers, 1992.

Cushing, Frank Hamilton. *Zuñi Folk Tales.* Tucson, Arizona: University of Arizona Press, 1986.

Feldman, Susan. *The Storytelling Stone: Traditional American Myths and Tales.* New York: Dell Publishing, 1991.

Locke, Raymond Friday. *Sweet Salt: Navajo Folktales and Mythology.* Santa Monica, California: Roundtable Publishing Company, 1990.

VanEtten, Teresa. *Ways of Indian Wisdom.* Santa Fe, New Mexico: Sunstone Press, 1987.

Tuck Everlasting

by Natalie Babbitt
New York: Farrar, Straus, and Giroux, 1975

The mysterious Tuck family keeps a secret about a spring whose water prevents them from ever growing older. When a ten-year-old girl and a malicious stranger discover their secret, the Tucks are confronted with an agonizing dilemma.

Topic Math as metaphor

Objective To build awareness of allusions to mathematics outside the content area

Applicable NCTM Standards 2, 3, 4, 12

Math Metaphors in Literature

1. In the first six pages of *Tuck Everlasting*, these geometry words or phrases are found:

fixed point	arc	axis	center of the wood
curves	square and solid	center of the earth	
angles	four feet high	acres	
tangent	narrowing dimension	edges	

2. See how many of these word references the students can find.

3. Discuss their meaning in the text and try to discover the author's purpose in using them.

4. As students continue reading the novel, have them keep track of all references to wheels, hubs, cycles, and so on. They should write down the direct quote and note its page number.

5. Ask these questions:

   a. To what is the author referring?

   b. Why? What is the author's intent?

   c. How does the wheel allusion tie in with the story line?

6. Challenge students to find other repeated images in their reading.

   a. What is the metaphor?

   b. What is the author's intent?

7. Begin a bulletin board or poster board display of references to mathematics that students find in other places—content areas, recreational reading, and so on.

8. Divide the display into sections:

   • Literal References

   • Metaphorical References

Flat Stanley

by Jeff Brown
New York: Dell Publishing, 1964

One morning Stanley Lambchop wakes up to find himself flattened. During the night a bulletin board has fallen on him. Not only does Stanley enjoy being flat, but has adventures that no other normal person could ever have.

A Wrinkle in Time

by Madeleine L'Engle
New York: Farrar, Straus, and Giroux, 1962

Meg, her brother Charles Wallace, and her friend Calvin O'Keefe search for Meg's missing father, a scientist who was involved in secret government work. They travel through time and space by means of the tesseract, a wrinkle in time, which allows travel in the fifth dimension.

Flatland: A Romance of Many Dimensions

by A Square (Edwin A. Abbott)
Boston: Little, Brown, 1899

Flatland is a two-dimensional world, a plane occupied by geometric shapes. No one there can envision or even imagine a three-dimensional world. After one of the squares returns from a visit to Spaceland, a land where solid shapes exist, he becomes an imprisoned heretic after he attempts to describe life there. Not surprisingly, the three-dimensional stranger who takes Square to Spaceland refuses to believe that a four-dimensional world exists because the idea is inconceivable.

Topic Comparing dimensions

Objectives To recognize, differentiate, and compare dimensions; expand thinking to envision or imagine dimensions

Applicable NCTM Standards 2, 3, 4, 12

Comparing Dimensions

Any of these lessons can be done independently of the other two books and they will work well even if the teacher has the only copy of the book(s).

If possible, read aloud to the students all of *Flat Stanley* and pertinent parts of *A Wrinkle in Time* and *Flatland* as denoted by the page numbers in the lessons. Hearing interesting portions of the latter two books can hook the students into reading them in their entirety on their own.

Flat Stanley

Read the book aloud and then ask these questions:

1. Stanley is flat. What does flat mean? What does two-dimensional mean? How are they similar? Different?

2. Is Stanley two-dimensional? What are his measurements? What does this prove?

3. Describe a world in which everything is flat. Then describe a two-dimensional world.

4. If you had not already known that the world is round, are there some clues that would prove to you that it is not flat?

5. Are there some questions or arguments you would have if everyone insisted the world is flat?

Sample ideas

- If you watch a ship sail into the horizon using a telescope, it doesn't shrink smaller and smaller until it disappears; it seems to sink on the horizon. Where does it go?

- If the ocean on both sides of the world goes to flat edges, why doesn't all the water run off leaving the earth dry?

A Wrinkle in Time

Read Chapter 5, "The Tesseract," to the students. Demonstrate the insect shortcut analogy (page 72).

1. Demonstrate the squaring of a line to make a square and the squaring of the square to make a cube.

- (a line) one dimension^2 = (a plane) the second dimension
- (a plane) second dimension^2 = (space) the third dimension
- (space) third dimension^2 = the fourth dimension (which is what?)
- fourth dimension^2 = the fifth dimension (which is what?)

This is fiction. The students may certainly have different theories about unknown dimensions.

2. What happens to Meg when she becomes two-dimensional (page 76)? Is anything similar to Flat Stanley's experience? When she becomes two-dimensional, how is Meg's experience more mathematically reasonable than Stanley's?

3. Mrs. Whatsit says that it is "rather amusing to be flat" (page 78). After Meg's experience, do your ideas about a two-dimensional world (from the *Flat Stanley* lesson) change?

4. Explain a time tesser (page 79).

5. Write what you think or understand about time being the fourth dimension.

6. Explain tesseracting in your own words.

Flatland

Since this book was written over 100 years ago (1870s–1880s), the language will seem archaic to the students. You will be more successful by reading the book first and then telling parts of the story to the students. This is fiction. Try to be as much a storyteller as a mathematician.

1. Include information such as this: In Flatland,

- All women are lines.

- Soldiers and the lowest-class workmen are isosceles triangles.

- Middle-class men are equilateral triangles.

- Professional men and gentlemen are squares and pentagons.

- Nobility begin as hexagons.

- Men can move up in classes as their number of sides and angles increases.

- When men become polygons with so many small sides that they cannot be distinguished from a circle, they are included in the highest class, the Priestly Order.

- The way men grow is by increasing in "intelligence, knowledge, and virtue" (page 10).

A Look at Society

The author says that women are seriously lacking "intelligence, knowledge, and virtue" and will always remain lines. "Once a woman, always a woman" (page 16). The author also states that women have no wit, sense, or conscience.

1. Discuss the author's viewpoint. When was this book written?   [Late 1800s] Where?   [England]   What were women's roles at that time? How were they treated by men?

2. At that same time in western America, women were becoming men's equals. They took strong roles on the farm and in business. Western states were the first to give women the right to vote and the first to send women to Congress. Why do you suppose this happened? How are women perceived today? How are they treated the same? Differently?

Dimension as Metaphor

1. What does it mean to have depth—depth of character, depth of personality?

2. When people say, "He's so one-dimensional," what do they mean?

Changing Perspective

1. How do the shapes in *Flatland* appear to each other (page 4)? For a demonstration, have students draw a large, thick-lined triangle. Standing at the edge of their desks, they view it from the top as:

    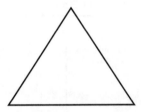

    As they gradually lower their eyes, the figure seems to flatten out:

    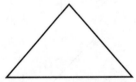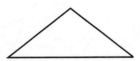

    But when their eyes are at table level, only a line segment appears:

    This is how all Flatlanders look to each other, like line segments.

2. Hand out copies of Figure 5.3 so students can practice changing the perspective on (transforming) polygons.

Figure 5.3 Reproducible
Transforming Polygons by Changing Perspective

Directions Draw the missing shape in each row.

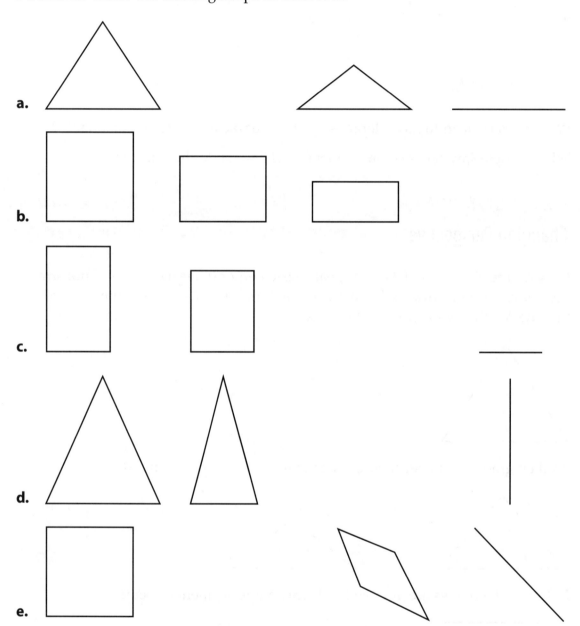

3. A stranger takes Square to a three-dimensional world called Spaceland. When Square sees the dimension of depth and solid form that he could not even imagine beforehand, he questions the stranger about the land of four dimensions (page 87). The stranger asserts that no such land exists because it is inconceivable. Square also begins to wonder about lands of five, six, seven, and eight dimensions.

> **a.** Why is he more able to believe in them than the stranger?
>
> **b.** Whose ideas are you more likely to believe? Why?

Related Books

Abbott, Edwin A. and Dionys Burger. *Flatland-Sphereland.* New York: HarperCollins, 1994.

Burger, Dionys. *Sphereland.* New York: HarperCollins, 1983.

Lowell, Susan. *The Boy With Paper Wings.* Minneapolis, Minnesota: Milkweed Editions, 1995.

Cathedral

by David Macaulay
Boston: Houghton Mifflin Company, 1973

The construction of the Gothic cathedral of Chutreaux is fictional, but it parallels the building of European Cathedrals in the twelfth through fourteenth centuries. This grand project is covered from the designing of the church through the final placing of sculptures in their niches—an 86-year-long endeavor.

Unbuilding

by David Macaulay

Boston: Houghton Mifflin Company, 1980

When the Empire State Building was completed in 1931, it was the tallest building in the world. Macaulay details how the building is unbuilt—dissembled piece by piece—until in 1993 nothing of it remains but a park and a monument.

Topic Geometry in architecture

Objective To recognize geometric form in architecture

Applicable NCTM Standards 1, 2, 3, 4, 7, 12

Geometric Form in Architecture

If possible, have multiple copies of these books around the room for students to read, or read them aloud to students. Be sure to show the illustrations on each page, perhaps using an opaque projector. (*Cathedral* is also available on videotape distributed by PBS. Check for it at your local library.) Discuss geometric forms continually. Choose any or all of the following instructions to give students.

Cathedral

1. Study the illustration on page 31 and list every geometric form you see. Tell where each form is located.

2. Do the same for the illustration on page 63.

3. Study the finished cathedral on pages 70 and 71. Write about all the ways you think geometry was used to construct this building.

4. Do you think that people spend this much time, energy, and money on construction of buildings these days? Explain your answer.

5. Find out who the great mathematicians were during the Middle Ages. In what ways did they change the field of geometry?

Unbuilding

1. On page 5, the author writes about the floor area in the Empire State Building. Look at the picture and answer these questions:

    a. What method would you use to find the floor area of this skyscraper? Remember, the floors are not all the same size. Explain your answer completely.

    b. What factors determined the building's floor area, shape, and height?

    c. List as many buildings as you can think of where the floors are different sizes.

    d. Why would it be necessary to know the building's total floor area?

2. On page 28, find the area of the grid. Round your measurements to the nearest centimeter (or inch). Explain all the steps you used to solve this problem. [You had to break the total area into two smaller areas, find the area of each, and then add them together.]

    a. Make copies of the Figures 5.4 (pages 155–156) in this book. Use the same process of separating into smaller areas and adding all the areas together to find the total area of the shapes in Figures 5.4.

    b. Use this same idea of dividing and conquering to find the volume of the shapes in Figure 5.5 on page 157.

    Answers to Figures 5.4

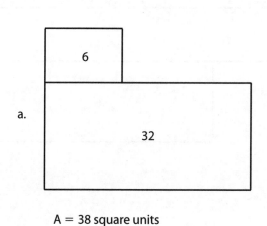

a.

A = 38 square units

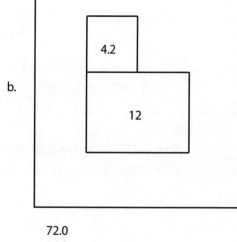

b.

72.0
−16.2
55.8   A = 55.8 square units

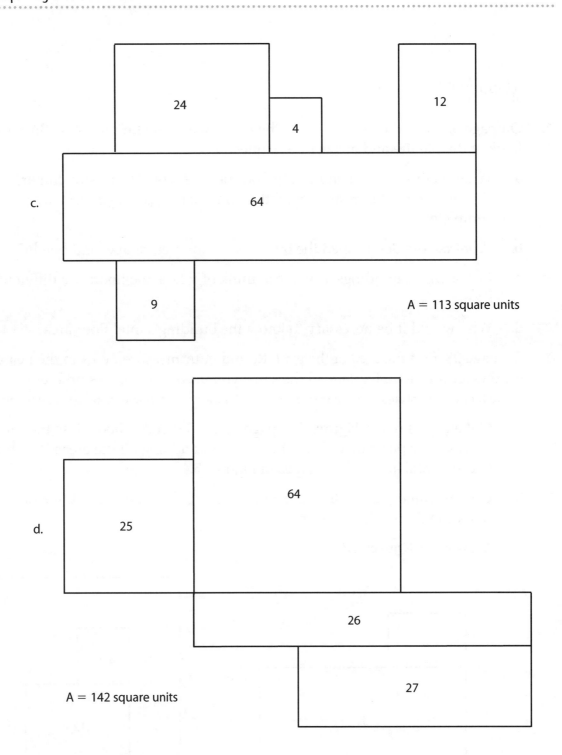

c.

24

4

12

64

9

A = 113 square units

d.

25

64

26

27

A = 142 square units

Answers to Figure 5.5

a. V = 58 cubic units; b. V = 324 cubic units

Figure 5.4 Reproducible
Divide and Conquer Area

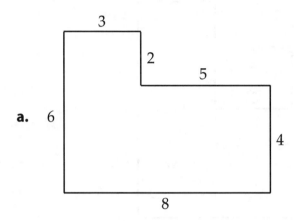

a.

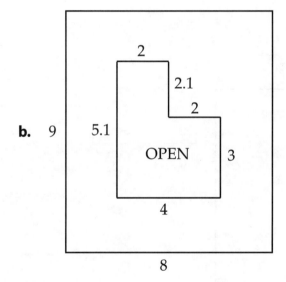

b.

Figure 5.4 Reproducible (continued)
Divide and Conquer Area

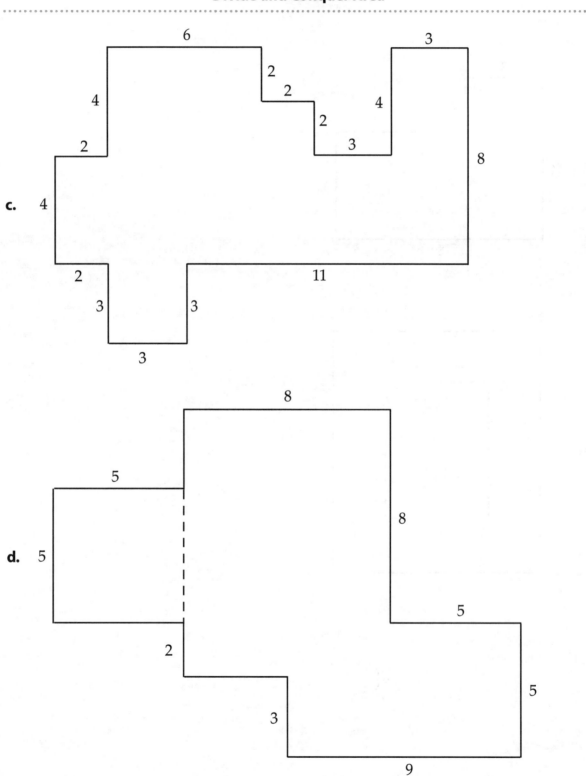

Figure 5.5 Reproducible
Divide and Conquer Volume

a.

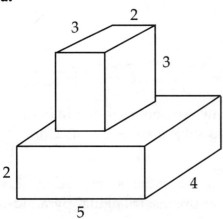

b.

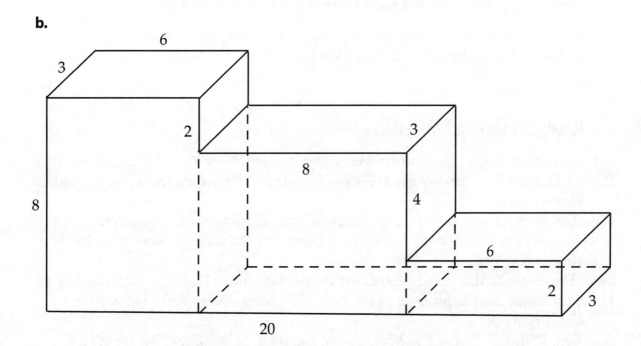

3. What is going on in pages 46 and 47 of *Unbuilding*? Why would a contractor need to figure out the surface area and perimeter of the building?

4. **Challenge** Determine the surface area of the shapes in Figure 5.5.

5. Be a critical reader. Explain at least two things about the book *Unbuilding* that just don't make sense.

Geometry in Architecture Activities

Study and classify forms. Fill the classroom with architecture books found in both the children and adult sections of the library. (Look-up subject areas: Architecture and Construction.)

1. Have students copy or trace and label geometric forms in the books, such as rectangles, rectangular prisms, triangles, triangular prisms, triangular pyramids, octagons, cylinders, symmetries, and so forth.

2. Have students copy or trace and label architectural forms from the books, such as columns, arches, obelisks, spires, buttresses, domes, and so on.

3. Ask the students to classify their drawings into categories (all the triangular prisms, all the spires, etc.) and create a poster for each category.

Related Books and Materials

Adams, Simon. *Explore the World of Man-Made Wonders*. New York: Golden Book, 1991.

Brown, David J. *The Random House Book of How Things Were Built*. New York: Random House, 1992.

Caselli, Giovanni. *Wonders of the World*. New York: Dorling Kindersley, 1992.

Eyewitness Visual Dictionaries. *The Visual Dictionary of Buildings*. New York: Dorling Kindersley, 1992.

Geis, Darlene, ed. *M.C. Escher: 29 Master Prints*. New York: Harry N. Abrams, 1983.

Hawkes, Nigel. *New Technology: Structures and Buildings*. New York: Twenty-First Century Books, 1994.

Isaacson, Philip M. *Round Buildings, Square Buildings, & Buildings That Wiggle Like a Fish*. New York: Alfred A. Knopf, 1988.

Macaulay, David. *Cathedral* (Video). Produced by Unicorn Projects, Inc. Distributed by PBS Video, 1988.

Macaulay, David. *Pyramid* (Video). Executive Producer, Ray Hubbard. Distributed by PBS Video, 1988.

Scholastic Staff. *Architecture and Construction*. New York: Scholastic, 1994.

Wilkinson, Philip. *Amazing Buildings*. New York: Dorling Kindersley, 1992.

Wood, Richard. *Architecture*. New York: Thompson Learning: 1995.

Measurement

The activities written for the first three novels presented in this chapter will provide students with the tools to calculate measurement, distance, and rate through the use of travel stories. The fourth book, *Julie of the Wolves*, will introduce them to measurement in other cultures. If you do not use or have access to these particular books, use the activities as models for any travel books you may be reading in your class.

Coast to Coast

by Betsy Byars
New York: Delacorte Press, 1992

Thirteen-year-old Birch convinces her grandfather to take her on a cross-country plane trip. They fly from South Carolina to California in her grandfather's antique Piper Cub.

Topics Tools of measurement, distance, and rate

Objective To use fictional long distance trips to calculate necessary travel information

Applicable NCTM Standards 1, 2, 4, 5, 6, 7, 13

Mapping Out a Trip

1. Pop and Birch use eight maps to plan their route from the Atlantic to the Pacific. Plan a cross-country trip for yourself by car.

    a. How many maps do you need to plot your trip?

    b. Mark your route on the map(s).

    c. How many miles will you travel?

2. After Pop and Birch get to Atlanta, they start following the interstate highway I-20.

   a. Why do they follow a road map for an air flight trip?   [The Piper Cub does not have sophisticated instrumentation, and because it is an old airplane, it flies low. The easiest way to navigate is to follow highways by sight.]

   b. What interstate are they on by the time they reach California?   [I-10]

   c. Which interstate highways would you travel on your trip?

3. Birch's mother made $2600 at the garage sale.

   a. How would you use that amount of money in your trip across America?

   b. Would it be enough to finance your trip?

4. Plan a budget.

   a. What are your expenses?   [sample answer: fuel—gas price × miles per gallon your car gets × distance]

   b. How many days will your trip take?

   c. How many meals will you eat?

   d. How much do you plan to spend per meal?

   e. What is your total food cost estimate?

   f. If you spend $50 per night for a motel room, how much will lodging cost?

   g. What other expenses will you have?

5. Where do Pop and Birch cross the Continental Divide?   [between Las Cruces and Lordsburg, New Mexico]

   a. Where will you cross it?

   b. What is the elevation there?

Understanding the Tools

On page 110, Birch is looking at a physical map and can tell how the terrain is climbing by the different colors on the map.

1. Using a physical map, describe how and where the land you will be driving through on your road trip changes.

2. List the measurement tools Birch and Pop used and note what is measured by each.

Answers

- Road maps: mileage

- Compass: direction (At this point you can teach compass skills. Or teach this when you work with circles in geometry: 0° is north; 90°, east; 180°, south; 270°, west. Note that 360° are used to mark off the increments, as in any circle.)

- Altimeter: feet above sea level (not feet above the *ground*). What is the difference? Why is that important?)

- Oil gauges: oil pressure and oil temperature

- Tachometer: how fast the engine is running

- Gas gauge: amount of gas (How does this work?)

- Air speed indicator: speed through the air

3. Birch says this about the air speed indicator: "Yes, but it always reads sixty-five or seventy when really we could be going forty-five miles an hour or ninety" (page 82). What does she mean?   [If they have wind blowing toward them, a head wind, the plane has to work hard to travel through the air, so the gauge may read seventy for air speed, but it actually might take them an hour to go 45 miles—45 mph. If they have a tail wind and are being blown along by it, the air speed indicator might read sixty, but the wind can push them faster to cover 90 miles in an hour—90 mph.]

Calculating Rate and Distance

1. The following formula is helpful to remember when working with travel problems: rate × time = distance or $rt = d$. Here is a simple example of how it works:

- A car has been traveling at 50 miles per hour (rate) for 4 hours (time). How far has it traveled (distance)?   [50 × 4 = 200 miles]

    The inverse operations are also applicable: distance divided by rate = time, or $d/r = t$, and distance divided by time = rate, or $d/t = r$.

- If a car is traveling 50 mph how long does it take to go 200 miles? [200 ÷ 50 = 4 hours]

- A car has traveled 200 miles in 4 hours. How fast is it going? [200 ÷ 4 = 50 mph]

2.   The Piper Cub's gas tank holds 12 gallons of gas. Birch thinks that they will run out of gas 2 miles before their next stop. Can you draw a diagram or illustration and write an explanation for the predicament written about on pages 92 and 93?

Sample of Student Work

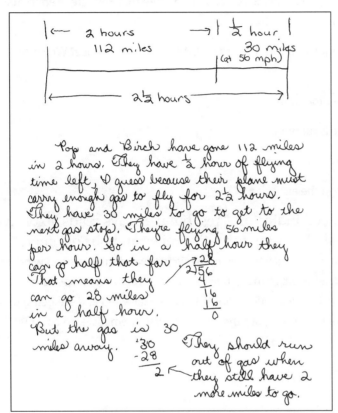

3.   On page 103 Birch has called home and is giving her dad details about today's flight: 380 miles in 6 hours and 28 minutes, using 26$\frac{1}{10}$ gallons of gas. How many miles per hour did they go? (Round 6 hours and 28 minutes to a figure easier to work with.)   [380 miles divided by 6.5 = 380 ÷ 65 ≈ 58.46 or ≈ 58 miles per hour. If students are not dividing by decimals yet, round the time down to 6 hours: 380 ÷ 6 = 63$\frac{1}{3}$ miles per hour.]

4.   How many miles did they go for each gallon of gas?   [To find miles per gallon, divide the number of miles traveled by the amount of gas used. Round the gallons to a figure easier to work with. 380 miles divided by 26 gallons ≈ 14.6 (14$\frac{8}{13}$) which is rounded up to 15 miles per gallon.]

5.   How many gallons per hour did they use?   [26 gallons divided by 6.5 hours = 4 gallons per hour. If 26 is divided by 6 even hours, the amount is 4$\frac{1}{3}$ gallons per hour.]

Wind Speed

The control tower says that the wind is blowing at about 20 knots, gusting to 25 or 30 (page 126). Pop tells Birch that's between 25 and 30 miles per hour. In 1805, Admiral Sir Francis Beaufort devised the following wind-speed scale which is still used today.

Description of Air	*Wind Speed*	
	mph	*Knots*
0. Calm	<1	<1
1. Light Air	1–3	1–3
2. Slight Breeze	4–7	4–6
3. Gentle Breeze	8–12	7–10
4. Moderate Breeze	13–18	11–16
5. Fresh Breeze	19–24	17–21
6. Strong Breeze	25–31	22–27
7. High Wind	32–38	38–33
8. Gale	39–46	34–40
9. Strong Gale	47–54	41–47
10. Whole Gale	55–63	48–55
11. Storm	64–75	56–65
12. Hurricane	>75	>65

1. What is the air called when it blows at about twenty knots?   [fresh breeze]

2. If the wind gusts to 25 or 30 knots and stays at that velocity, what kind of wind is it?   [strong breeze to high wind]

3. Is Pop's answer that 20 knots is between 25 and 30 miles per hour okay? Why?
[Yes. Pop's answer is an estimate—it's close enough. He's under pressure and frustrated. In this particular case it really does not make any difference, and it is an adequate answer to quiet Birch.]

4. Name other situations where "close enough" estimates are acceptable.

5. Yesterday (page 153) they traveled 410 miles and used 27.2 gallons of gas. About how many miles per gallon did they get?   [410 miles divided by 27 ≈ 15 miles per gallon]

Compare and Contrast

While crossing the San Gabriel Mountains in California, Birch says, "When I look at mountains like that, I get a new respect for pioneers, don't you?" (page 155).

1. What does she mean?

2. Compare and contrast three transcontinental trips: Pop and Birch's plane trip, the imaginary excursion you planned to drive across the United States, and a pioneer's exodus from the East to the West Coast.

3. If Pop had been born 200 years earlier, do you think he would have been a pioneer? Why? Read what Birch says about him on pages 96 and 97.

4. Read pioneer books such as *Go West, Young Women!* by Kathleen Karr (1996).

The Petticoat Party, Book 1
Go West, Young Women!

by Kathleen Karr
New York: HarperCollins Publisher, 1996

The Brown family travels from Massachusetts to Oregon in 1846. During their wagon train journey, disaster befalls the men in the party. The women must rely on their own strengths and resources to complete the journey. This is the story of twelve-year-old Phoebe, her sister and mother, and the other pioneering women of the wagon train.

More Distance Calculations

1. The oxen-pulled wagons in the Brown family's party travelled about 15 miles per day (page 21).

    a. What is located about 15 miles from your house?

    b. How long does it take you to get there?

    c. How far can you travel in one day?

2. Gunpowder was made of 75% saltpeter, 10% sulphur, and 15% charcoal (page 31). Sketch these percentages on a circle graph. Do not use computation or a protractor. [Students should be familiar with common percentages and their fraction equivalents: 75% = ³/₄, and 25% (percentages of sulphur and charcoal combined) = ¹/₄. In the circle graph, ³/₄ of the circle is saltpeter and ¹/₄ is sulphur and charcoal. The charcoal gets a little over half of that fourth.]

Example

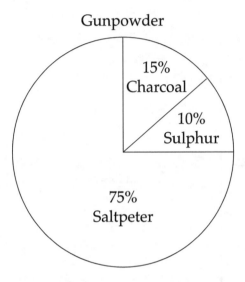

Gunpowder

15% Charcoal

10% Sulphur

75% Saltpeter

3. Pioneers could not accurately measure time and distance, so their rates were not exact: "It was more than a hundred endless miles closer to Laramie and a good week later …" (page 73).

   a. Estimate their rate of travel.

   b. What value will you use for "more than a hundred miles"? [Sample answer: 110 miles]

   c. What is "a good week"? [Sample answers: At least a week, or a little over a week; one estimated answer could be 110 miles divided by 8 days = 13³/₄ miles, or about 13–14 miles per day.]

4. Every night Phoebe "would scratch another fourteen or fifteen or even sixteen miles" from their total mileage. They are 75 miles from Chimney Rock (pages 92–94).

   a. How many days will it take them to get there? [75 miles ÷ 15 miles per day = 5 days.]

   b. How long would it take you to travel 75 miles? [In a car going 75 mph, it would take one hour.]

5.   Read page 96 and determine Phoebe's concern.

   a.   What is she calculating? Show her (and your) work.

   b.   What does the answer mean?

Sample of Student Work

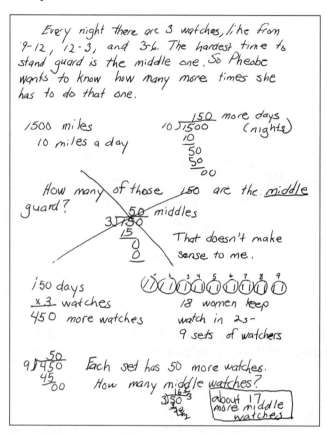

6.   It is 4 or 5 more days to Fort Laramie (page 141).

   a.   How many more miles is that?   [Four or five days can be averaged as 4.5 more days. They can travel between 10 and 15 miles a day: $4.5 \times 10 = 45$ and $4.5 \times 15 = 67.5$ or ≈ 67. It is between 45 and 67 miles to Fort Laramie.]

7.   Phoebe says that it is seventy yards across Horse Creek (page 168).

   a.   How many feet is that?   [$70 \times 3 = 210$ feet]

   b.   What else do you know that is 70 yards?   [seven 10-yard markers of a football field—$^7/_{10}$ of the field.]

   c.   How far away is 70 yards away in your school yard?

   d.   Have you ever seen a creek 70 yards wide?

8. After Fort Laramie, it is still another 1400 miles to Oregon (page 173).

    a. About how long will it take the wagon train to get there?   [If you figure that they travel approximately 12 miles a day, the 1400 miles should be divided by that rate— 1400 ÷ 12 ≈ 117 days.]

    b. How many months is that?   [117 days divided by 30 days per month is 3.9 ($3^9/_{10}$), or about 4 months.]

9. If they are still traveling when it is November, what else could slow them down? [cold weather, snow, lack of food]

10. Look for other measurement and mathematics applications in other travel books, such as *Around the World in Eighty Days* by Jules Verne.

Around the World in Eighty Days

by Jules Verne
New York: William Morrow, 1988

Phileas Fogg bets that he can travel around the world in eighty days. He travels by boat, rail, and even elephant, and although he suffers many setbacks, Phileas Fogg returns to England in the nick of time to win his bet.

Budgeting Time

Phileas Fogg kept his life obsessively scheduled (page 9). "Seen in the various phases of his daily life, he gave the idea of being perfectly well-balanced, as exactly regulated as a Leroy chronometer." If this passage were written in modern times, Verne might have written that Fogg was as regulated as an atomic clock.

1. Look up information on the atomic clock.

    a. How does it keep time?

    b. How accurate is it?

    c. Who needs time to be measured so precisely?

2. Fogg was meticulous about the way he spent time and always had time for everything that needed to be done. He was never late (page 9).

   a.   What is it in your life that you just don't have time for? Homework? Practice? Chores?

   b.   Write out your daily schedule—how you spend all your waking hours— and find the space (It's there!) when you can do that activity.

3. What are you always late for?

   a.   List the steps it takes you to get ready for that.

   b.   Where can you be more deliberate and prepare earlier, save steps, or hurry the process?

   c.   Challenge yourself to be punctual.

More Travel Estimations

The London newspapers printed stories about the amazing upcoming excursion and even printed a schedule that could be used to accomplish the feat (*Around the World in Eighty Days*, pages 16–17):

From London to Suez via Mont Cenis and Brindisi, by rail and steamboats	7 days
From Suez to Bombay, by steamer	13 days
From Bombay to Calcutta, by rail	3 days
From Calcutta to Hong Kong, by steamer	13 days
From Hong Kong to Yokohama (Japan), by steamer	6 days
From Yokohama to San Francisco, by steamer	22 days
From San Francisco to New York, by rail	7 days
From New York to London, by steamer and rail	9 days
Total	**80 days**

1. What is the distance around the world—its circumference?   [At the equator the circumference is 24,901.46 miles or 39,842.336 kilometers.]

2. Fogg travels around the world and goes 26,000 miles. What accounts for the difference?   [He does not travel in a straight line along the equator.]

3. How many kilometers is 26,000 miles?   [26,000 × 1.6 = 41,600 kilometers]

4. Fogg is confident that he will make all his connections on time. How can he make up for it if he doesn't?

5. Do you have a bus system in your city? Get bus schedules and plan a trip across town. Plan a difficult route that requires transferring busses.

    a. Are all the connecting times close?

    b. What happens if you are one minute late?

    c. How long is the delay?

    d. Are there alternative routes?

    e. Do you have a back-up plan?

6. These are the terms of Fogg's bet (page 19): He bets £20,000 (pounds) that he will successfully tour the world in 80 days (or 1920 hours or 115,200 minutes). At 1998 exchange rates, how many U.S. dollars is £20,000? (Have students find today's exchange rates for more timely calculations.)
[$1.00 = £1.53; 20,000 × 1.53 = $30,600]

7. Fogg knows the time breakdown for 80 days. In the months of June and July combined, how many hours are there? Minutes?   [61 days = 1464 hours or 87,840 minutes.]

8. Fogg kept an accurate travel schedule in his notebook which, at the end of his first week, concluded: "Total hours spent, 158½; or in days, six days and a half" (page 35).

    a. How many days are in 200 hours?   [200 ÷ 24 = 8⅓ days]

    b. How many hours are in 75 days?   [75 × 24 = 1800 hours]

9. Because they departed in such haste, Passepartout, Fogg's servant, forgot to turn off his gas-burner at home. Wasting gas, he loses two shillings every four and twenty hours.

    a. How much does he lose on wasted fuel before he gets home?
    [2 shillings × 80 days = 160 shillings]

    b. How many pounds is that?   [20 shillings = £1.00, so 160 shillings = £8.00]

    c. Is this something that should be memorized?   [Not really. It is information that can easily be looked up. And shillings were discontinued in 1971.]

Calculating Land Formations

The shape of India is described as a "great reversed triangle of land, with its base in the north and its apex in the south … fourteen hundred thousand square miles …" (page 46).

1. What is another way of saying fourteen hundred thousand?   [1,400,000—one million four-hundred thousand.]

2. If India were not shaped like a triangle, how many different dimensions of the country that would have an area of 1,400,000 square miles can you come up with?   [The different combinations of length and breadth of a rectangular shape are the same as the area's factors. Examples: 1 × 1,400,000; 2 × 700,000; 4 × 350,000; 100 × 14,000; 1000 × 1400, etc.]

3. If India were square, what would its dimensions be?   [Find the square root of 1,400,000 on a calculator: 1183.2159 miles on each side.]

4. How do you find the area of a triangle?   [½ base × height or ½ bh]   Now come up with some possible dimensions of India as a triangle—½ of its base (which runs east and west at the north) multiplied by its height (distance from north to south). [These products must be twice as much as 1,400,000—2,800,000—because they will be halved to the area of 1,400,000 square miles, 1/2bh. Sample answers: 2000 × 1400, 3500 × 800, 1000 × 2800, etc.]

5. It is possible to find a figure's area by counting square units and half units inside the figure. Make a copy of Figure 6.1 for every student. Find the area of the shapes on Figure 6.1.   [Answers: a. 14 square units; b. 20 square units; c. 19 square units; d. 8 square units; e. 14½ square units; f. 18 square units; g. 13 square units; h. 18½ square units]

6. Make a copy of dot paper, Figure 6.2, for every student. On a clean sheet of dot paper, draw eight different shapes that have the same areas as the answers in the above exercise.

Time and Travel

1. The trip from Calcutta to Hong Kong via steamer, about 3500 miles, takes from 10 to 12 days to complete (page 91). Approximately how many miles per day will they travel?   [10–12 days averages as 11 days; $d \div t = r$; $3500 \div 11 \approx 318$ miles per day]

2. The distance from San Francisco to New York by rail is 3786 miles and takes 7 days (page 162). What is the rate?   [≈ 541 miles per day]   Why is this much faster? [Traveling by train is faster than traveling by steamer.]

Figure 6.1 Reproducible
Figuring Area by Counting Square Units and Half Units

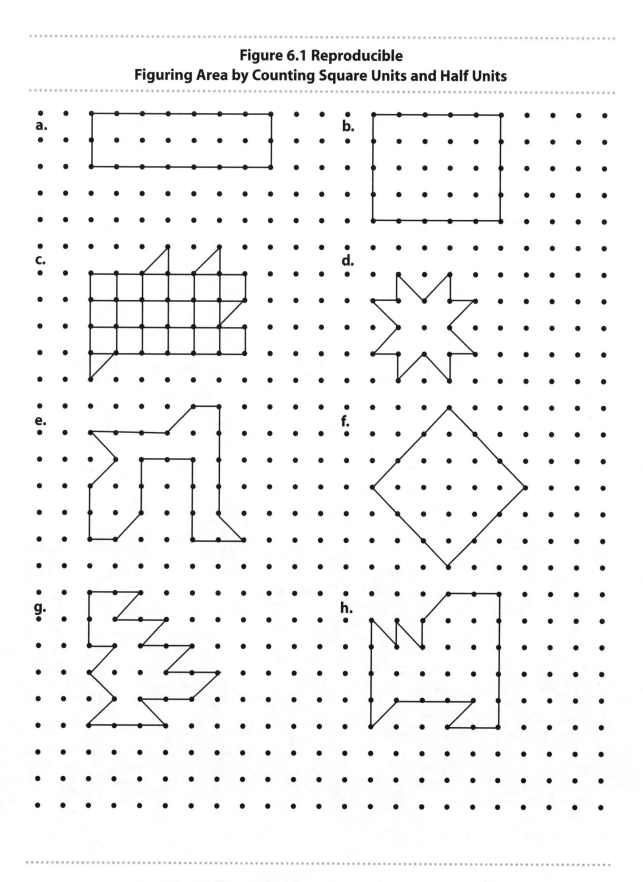

Figure 6.2 Reproducible
Dot Paper

3. The distance from San Francisco to Denver by rail is 1382 miles and takes 3 days (page 184). What is the rate?   [≈ 461 miles per day]

4. Fogg traveled the 200 mile distance between Fort Kearney and Omaha in 5 hours.

    a. What is the rate?   [40 miles per hour]

    b. A mere 26 years earlier, how long would it have taken Phoebe Brown's wagon train to travel the same distance?   [200 miles ÷ 12 miles per day ≈ 17 days]

5. How do you account for the great difference in rate?   [Phoebe traveled by oxen-pulled wagon. Fogg traveled in a sledge—a huge sled with sails on it. The ground was frozen and the wind strong. He got blown along at 40 miles per hour.]

6. How many knots were they traveling?   [See the chart on page 163; between 34 and 40 knots.]

7. The ship to Liverpool traveled between 11 and 12 knots (page 209). About how many miles per hour is that?   [13–18 mph]

8. After Fogg's arrival in London, why did he think he had lost the bet? Explain in detail.

9. What would have been the result if Fogg had traveled around the world going west, starting in the United States, instead of going toward the east?

Julie of the Wolves

by Jean Craighead George
New York: Harper and Row, 1972

While running away from home and an unwanted marriage, thirteen-year-old Miyax becomes lost on the North Slope of Alaska. While lost without tools or instruments, Miyax (Julie) figures time throughout the Arctic's continuous winter night and the summer's neverending daylight. She can determine date, month, season, location, and temperature. (Although this is an interesting aspect of the book, students should not be mislead that it is the author's emphasis.) Eventually she is befriended by a wolf pack. Helped by the wolves and her father's training, Miyax struggles daily for survival.

Students should read the book straight through for literary enjoyment and to gain an appreciation for the rich traditions of Eskimo life. Only afterward should they be given the measurement questions.

Topic Measurement in other cultures

Objective To discover alternative methods of measurement

NCTM Standards 1, 2, 3, 4, 6, 7, 13

 Measuring Time

Hours

1. What time is it on page 5? What two clues does Miyax use to determine this?

2. Why is it difficult to measure the passing of time (page 27)? The author writes that "time in the Arctic was the rhythm of life." Give examples to explain what this means.

3. How long is the night (page 43)? When do the tundra animals sleep?

4. When is Miyax trying to sleep? (page 49) Explain the meaning of the statement, "The sun reached its apogee."

Days

5. Note the author's use of the phrases "two sleeps ago" (page 5), "many sleeps" (page 6), and "exactly seven sleeps ago" (page 10). Why isn't time recorded as "days"? Or as "nights ago"?

6. How is Julie determining the passage of time (page 153)?

Months

7. Read page 61 and answer these questions: What is the month and week? How does Miyax know? Explain the author's meaning. What day is it on the wolf pup's calendar?

8. Miyax remembers an incident from one September (page 81). What are the clues for the month? What do these clues mean?

Seasons

9. Miyax says, "I am lost and the sun will not set for a month. There is no North Star to guide me" (page 10). What season is it?

10. Which season approaches on page 38? How does Miyax know?

11. What season is it on page 50? What is the clue?

12. What season is approaching on page 62? What are the clues? What does are the consequences of the approaching season? Why is Miyax worried?

13. Miyax knows what season it is and the exact date on pages 64–65. How does she know these things? How will Miyax know when it is November 21? What will the next 3 months be like?

14. What is the significance of January 24 (page 100)? Describe the day. How long does it last?

15. What's the date on page 147? the season? the duration? the characteristics? Explain what Miyax's days will be like now.

Determining Location

1. The author describes the "cosmos" in which Miyax is lost (page 6). Figure out the square mileage of this area. Describe it.

2. How could Miyax get lost after travelling a mere quarter mile (page 30)? How far would this be from your school? How does she find her way back to her camp?

3. The tundra looks the same in every direction (page 30). What clues could have told her the way north?

4. How does Miyax attempt to get her directional bearings (page 54)? Draw a sketch similar to the one Miyax drew in the soil. Label Fairbanks and Point Hope.

5. What new clues does Miyax use to make a compass (page 69)? Add the new details to your sketch.

6. Now how does Miyax determine her direction (pages 118, 126)? Where will it lead her?

7. She can find her location more accurately now (pages 129–130). How?

8. How can Miyax tell where the wilderness ends and civilization begins (page 134)? What are her reactions?

9. How is Miyax finding her way (page 150)? How accurate is her method?

Metaphorical Time

1. Miyax's father had told her, "The hour of the lemming is over for four years" (page 14). What does he mean by the "hour" of the lemming?

2. It is Julie's time to be married (page 89). What was the time for an Eskimo girl to marry? How will you decide when it is your time to get married?

3. "The hour of the wolf and the Eskimo is over" (page 170). Why? What does this mean?

Temperature

How does Miyax figure the temperature (page 138)? Describe three ways you could estimate the temperature in three different settings and seasons.

Time in Other Cultures

The following information can be shared with students or used as jumping-off points for research projects.

- In ancient Egypt, the year was divided into 12 months. Each month had three 10-day weeks. Three seasons, each with 4 months, made a year.

- The Egyptians measured hours from sunrise to sunset, then from sunset to sunrise. Therefore, "hours" would be different lengths at different times of the year. In summer, day hours were longer and night hours were shorter. In winter, a day hour would be shorter and the night hour longer.

- Egyptians used water clocks. Water dripped at a constant rate into a container with markings at different water levels. Each level corresponded to an hour passing.

  1. Research what other people used a water clock. Who is thought to have invented it?

- Ancient cultures in prehistoric England built circles of huge stones. The most famous remaining circle is Stonehenge. A huge rock called the Heelstone lies outside the circle. The line that runs from the center of the circle to the Heelstone points to the rising sun on the longest day of the year, June 21, also called the summer solstice.

2. Have students research ancient cultures in other parts of the world with similar structures.

- The modern measure of a year is 365.2422 days. Ancient Mayan Indians measured the year to be 365.242 days long.

  3. Have students research the Mayas to find what methods they used to gauge so accurately the passage of time.

- Not even all contemporary cultures keep time the same way. In east Africa, some societies measure their days from sunrise—6:00 A.M.—which they call 12:00. Their 1:00 A.M. is our 7:00 A.M.

  4. Have students make a chart of their daily schedule using sunrise time.

- The Islamic year is based on the cycle of the moon's phases. Their calendar months alternate between 29 and 30 days because a lunar phase is about 29.5 days long. The Islamic year is 354 days long. The numbering of years began in A.D. 622.

  5. Can you figure out the Islamic year by subtracting 622 from our present year? Why? How could we calculate it?

  6. Have students research ancient calendars such as the Aztec calendar.

  7. Compare and contrast calendars (e.g., Aztec, Hebrew, Islamic, Western).

  8. **For interested students:** Find the differences between a sidereal year, a tropical year, a lunar year, and an anomalistic year.

Mathematical Systems in Other Ages

Today we use a base-ten mathematics system. In the decimal system, we count in units of ten. The ancient Sumerians and Babylonians counted in units of sixty—a sexagesimal system. It is not strictly sexagesimal because the system uses factors of 10 as well as 6—that is, 1, 10, 60, 600, 3600, 36,000, and so on. The Mesopotamians later adopted this mathematical system.

1. A base-60 system is easy to use because 60 can be divided evenly by so many numbers.

   a. How many are there?   [12]

   b. What are they? That is, find all the factors of 60.

2. Sexagesimal counting remains with us today. Circles are marked off in 360 degrees. Dials of clocks and watches are divided into 60s. Sixty minutes makes one hour; 60 seconds, a minute.

These are the notation symbols used in Sumerian math:

D	1	$\bigcirc$	10
$\mathrm{D}\,\mathrm{D}$	2	D	60
$\mathrm{D}\,\mathrm{D}\,\mathrm{D}$	3		600
$\begin{matrix}\mathrm{D}\,\mathrm{D}\\\mathrm{D}\,\mathrm{D}\end{matrix}$	4	$\bigcirc$	3600
$\begin{matrix}\mathrm{D}\,\mathrm{D}\,\mathrm{D}\\\mathrm{D}\,\mathrm{D}\end{matrix}$	5	$\bigodot$	36,000

Have students write other numbers with Sumerian symbols and convert them to decimal system equivalents using expanded notation.

Example

$$\bigcirc \mathrm{D}\,\mathrm{D}\,\mathrm{D}\,\bigcirc\bigcirc\bigcirc\begin{matrix}\mathrm{D}\,\mathrm{D}\\\mathrm{D}\,\mathrm{D}\end{matrix} = (1 \times 3600) + (2 \times 60) + (3 \times 10) + (4 \times 1)$$

$$= 3600 + 120 + 30 + 4 = 3754$$

3. In 1792 when French mathematicians were developing the metric system, they devised decimal timekeeping. A week was 10 days long and was named a decade. Three decades made a month. Every day had 10 hours, with 100 minutes in an hour and 100 seconds in a minute. Have students defend or refute the system.

Related Books

Adams, Simon. *Man-Made Wonders.* New York: Golden Books, 1991.

Aven, Anthony F. *Empires of Time: Calendars, Clocks, and Cultures.* New York: Basic Books, 1989.

Burns, Marilyn. *This Book Is About Time.* Boston: Little, Brown and Company, 1978.

Coblence, Jean-Michel. *The Earliest Cities.* Morristown, New Jersey: Silver Burdett, 1987.

Crosher, Judith. *Ancient Egypt.* New York: Viking, 1993.

Hall, Elizabeth. *Child of the Wolves.* Boston: Houghton Mifflin, 1996.

Hobbs, Will. *Kokopelli's Flute.* New York: Atheneum Books for Young Readers, 1995.

Kramer, Samuel Noah. *The Sumerians: Their History, Culture, and Character.* Chicago: University of Chicago Press, 1963.

McIntosh, Jane. *Archeology.* New York: Alfred A. Knopf, 1994.

Ross, Catherine Sheldrick. *Circles.* Reading, Massachusetts: Addison Wesley Publishing Company, 1993.

Zindel, Paul. *The Doom Stone.* New York: HarperCollins, 1995.

Appendix

NCTM Standards for School Mathematics

The National Council of Teachers of Mathematics created the Standards for School Mathematics* as a means of providing goals for curriculum and evaluation. The standards are not meant to be study units or chapters of textbooks. Instead, they should be used to incorporate ideas and topics across standards.

Standard 1: Mathematics as Problem Solving In grades 5–8, the mathematics curriculum should include numerous and varied experiences with problem solving as a method of inquiry and application so that students can

- use problem-solving approaches to investigate and understand mathematical content;
- formulate problems from situations within and outside mathematics;
- develop and apply a variety of strategies to solve problems, with emphasis on multistep and nonroutine problems;
- verify and interpret results with respect to the original problem situation;
- generalize solutions and strategies to new problem situations;
- acquire confidence in using mathematics meaningfully.

Standard 2: Mathematics as Communication In grades 5–8, the study of mathematics should include opportunities to communicate so that students can

- model situations using oral, written, concrete, pictorial, graphical, and algebraic methods;
- reflect on and clarify their own thinking about mathematical ideas and situations;
- develop common understandings of mathematical ideas, including the role of definitions;
- use the skills of reading, listening, and viewing to interpret and evaluate mathematical ideas;
- discuss mathematical ideas and make conjunctures and convincing arguments;
- appreciate the value of mathematical notation and its role in the development of mathematical ideas.

Standard 3: Mathematics as Reasoning In grades 5–8, reasoning shall permeate the mathematics curriculum so that the students can

- recognize and apply deductive and inductive reasoning;

- understand and apply reasoning processes, with special attention to spatial reasoning and reasoning with proportions and graphs;

- make and evaluate mathematical conjectures and arguments;

- validate their own thinking;

- appreciate the pervasive use and power of reasoning as a part of mathematics.

Standard 4: Mathematical Connections In grades 5–8, the mathematics curriculum should include the investigation of mathematical connections so that students can

- see mathematics as an integrated whole;

- explore problems and describe results using graphical, numerical, physical, algebraic, and verbal mathematical models or representations;

- use mathematical ideas to further their understanding of other mathematical ideas;

- apply mathematical thinking and modeling to solve problems that arise in other disciplines, such as art, music, psychology, science, and business;

- value the role of mathematics in our culture and society.

Standard 5: Number and Number Relationships In grades 5–8, the mathematics curriculum should include the continued development of number and number relationships so that students can

- understand, represent, and use numbers in a variety of equivalent forms (integer, fraction, decimal, percent, exponential, and scientific notation) in real-world and mathematical problem situations;

- develop number sense for whole numbers, fractions, decimals, integers, and rational numbers;

- understand and apply ratios, proportions, and percents in a wide variety of situations;

- investigate relationships among fractions, decimals, and percents;

- represent numerical relationships in one- and two-dimensional graphs.

Standard 6: Number Systems and Number Theory In grades 5–8, the mathematics curriculum should include the study of number systems and number theory so that students can

- understand and appreciate the need for numbers beyond the whole numbers;

- develop and use order relations for whole numbers, fractions, decimals, integers, and rational numbers;

- extend their understanding of whole number operations, to fractions, decimals, integers, and rational numbers;

- understand how the basic arithmetic operations are related to one another;
- develop and apply number theory concepts (e.g., primes, factors, and multiples) in real-world and mathematical problem situations.

Standard 7: Computation and Estimation In grades 5–8, the mathematics curriculum should develop the concepts underlying computation and estimation in various contexts so that students can

- compute with whole numbers, fractions, decimals, integers, and rational numbers;
- develop, analyze, and explain procedures for computation and techniques for estimation;
- develop, analyze, and explain methods for solving proportions;
- select and use an appropriate method for computing from among mental arithmetic, paper-and-pencil, calculator, and computer methods;
- use computation, estimation, and proportion to solve problems;
- use estimation to check the reasonableness of results.

Standard 8: Patterns and Functions In grades 5–8, the mathematics curriculum should include explorations of patterns and functions so that the students can

- describe, extend, analyze, and create a wide variety of patterns;
- describe and represent relationships with tables, graphs, and rules;
- analyze functional relationships to explain how a change in one quantity results in a change in another;
- use patterns and functions to represent and solve problems.

Standard 9: Algebra In grades 5–8, the mathematics curriculum should include explorations of algebraic concepts and processes so that students can

- understand the concepts of variable, expression, and equation;
- represent situations and number patterns with tables, graphs, verbal rules, and equations and explore the interrelationships of these representations;
- analyze tables and graphs to identify properties and relationships;
- develop confidence in solving linear equations using concrete, informal, and formal methods;
- investigate inequalities and nonlinear equations informally;
- apply algebraic methods to solve a variety of real-world and mathematical problems.

Standard 10: Statistics In grades 5–8, the mathematics curriculum should include exploration of statistics in real-world situations so that students can

- systematically, collect, organize, and describe data;
- construct, read, and interpret tables, charts, and graphs;

- make inferences and convincing arguments that are based on data analysis;
- evaluate arguments that are based on data analysis;
- develop an appreciation for statistical methods as powerful means for decision making.

Standard 11: Probability In grades 5–8, the mathematics curriculum should include exploration of probability in real-world situations so that students can

- model situations by devising and carrying out experiments or simulations to determine probabilities;
- model situations by constructing a sample space to determine probabilities;
- appreciate the power of using a probability model by comparing experimental results with mathematical expectations;
- make predictions that are based on experimental or theoretical probabilities;
- develop and appreciation for the pervasive use of probability in the real world.

Standard 12: Geometry In grades 5–8, the mathematics curriculum should include the study of the geometry of one, two, and three dimensions in a variety of situations so that students can

- identify, describe, compare, and classify geometric figures;
- visual and represent geometric figures with special attention to developing spatial sense;
- explore transformations of geometric figures;
- represent and solve problems using geometric models;
- understand and apply geometric properties and relationships;
- develop and appreciation of geometry as a means of describing the physical world.

Standard 13: Measurement In grades 5–8, the mathematics curriculum should include extensive concrete experiences using measurement so that students can

- extend their understanding of the process of measurement;
- estimate, make, and use measurements to describe and compare phenomena;
- select appropriate units and tools to measure to the degree of accuracy required in a particular situation;
- understand the structure and use of systems of measurement;
- extend their understanding of the concepts of perimeter, area, volume, angle measure, capacity, and weight and mass;
- develop the concepts of rates and other derived and indirect measurements;
- develop formulas and procedures for determining measures to solve problems.

Index